Ultimate Sailing Adventures
100 Extraordinary Experiences on the Water

Miles Kendall

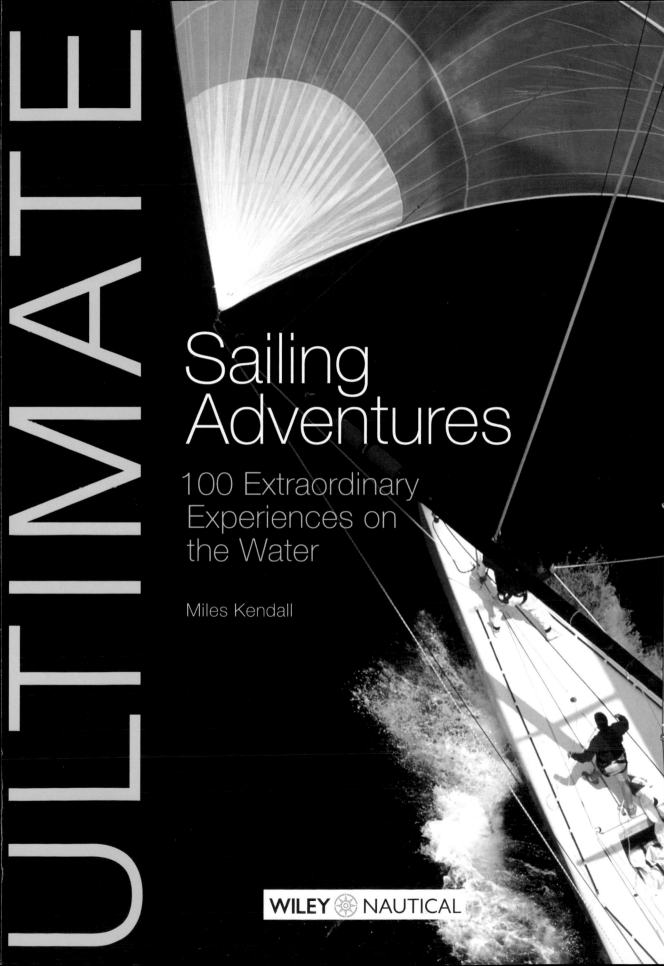

ULTIMATE

Sailing Adventures

100 Extraordinary Experiences on the Water

Miles Kendall

WILEY ✦ NAUTICAL

A catalogue record for this book is available from the British Library.

ISBN: 978-0-470-74697-4

Set in 8.2/9.8 ITC Garamond by Laserwords Private Ltd. Chennai, India
Printed in China by SNP Leefung Printers Ltd

Dedication

In memory of my father, who taught me how to sail.

Contents

Conversions

For clarity, throughout the book all measurements, distances, etc., are given in metric only. Please refer to the following conversion information to obtain the imperial equivalent.

To convert *to* metric, multiply by the factor shown.
To convert *from* metric, divide by the factor.

Length

miles: kilometres	1.6093
feet: metres	0.3048
inches: millimetres	25.4
inches: centimetres	2.54

Area

square miles: square kilometres	2.59
square feet: square metres	0.0929
square feet: square centimetres	929.03
square inches: square millimetres	645.16
square inches: square centimetres	6.4516

Weight

tons: kilograms	1016.05
tons: tonnes	1.0160
pounds: kilograms	0.4536

Temperature

Multiply	by	to get
°F Fahrenheit	$- 32 \times 5 \div 9$	°C Celsius
°C Celsius	$\times 9 \div 5 + 32$	°F Fahrenheit

category
voyages and destinations

location
Southern Ocean

difficulty
extreme

time
14 days

tempted by this?
try sailing through the Northwest Passage

FOLLOW IN SHACKLETON'S WAKE

Do you dare take on the greatest nautical adventure?

The greatest adventures are those that are a matter of life and death where the odds seem impossibly stacked against success. That was certainly the case when Ernest Shackleton set off in a small boat to cross hundreds of kilometres of the gale-whipped Southern Ocean in a bid to save the crew of Endurance. It is possibly the greatest marine adventure of all time and one that a few brave souls have tried to replicate in recent times.

The drama started in January 1915 when Endurance became stuck in ice as she sailed towards Antarctica. The plan was to land Shackleton and his team of explorers so that they could attempt the first crossing of the frozen continent. With the ship trapped, there was nothing to do but stay onboard as the moving ice carried her north for ten months. The ship was abandoned on 27 October, and finally crushed by the pressure of the frozen sea on 21 November.

Shackleton and the 28 crew of the Endurance camped out on the ice until that broke up beneath them and they took to three small open boats that had been carried on deck. Three days later they made landfall on the rocky shore of Elephant Island. It was the first time the men had stood on dry land in 14 months but the island was uninhabited and barren. To stay there would mean eventual starvation.

The closest possible salvation lay on South Georgia, a mountainous island 1280 km away that was used as a base for whaling vessels. Shackleton prepared the largest of the boats, James Caird, by improvising a deck and loading her with ballast to stop her being capsized in the high winds and mountainous seas that race across the frozen Southern Ocean.

The epic passage to South Georgia is the stuff of legend. Water froze on deck, threatening to tip the boat over and freak waves bore down on the tiny craft. The bailing was constant and the discomfort unimaginable. After 14 harrowing days at sea the crew landed in a little cove on South Georgia – but death was now closer than ever for they had to cross a frozen mountain ridge if they were to reach civilization and rescue. That 27-km trek saw them reach an altitude of 1,350 metres and was completed by men who were half-starved and had none of the modern equipment or clothing available today. They eventually stumbled into the tiny settlement and their ordeal was finally over. The men left on Elephant Island were then rescued, 105 days after landing there.

The story of Shackleton's Trans-Antarctic expedition has inspired generation after generation of adventurers and several have followed in his wake, using replica boats, though supported by modern technology and back-up teams.

If such a journey seems a little extreme, consider booking a berth on one of the expedition charter yachts that sail the Antarctic waters and call in at Elephant Island and South Georgia. Some even carry climbers who attempt to follow Shackleton's route across the island – though the trek is considered simply too dangerous for many.

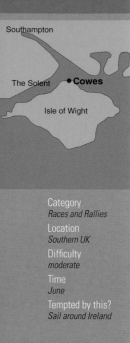

Southampton

The Solent • Cowes

Isle of Wight

Category
Races and Rallies

Location
Southern UK

Difficulty
moderate

Time
June

Tempted by this?
Sail around Ireland

JOIN BRITAIN'S BIGGEST RACE

The Round the Island Race is a true sailing spectacular

If you are only ever going to take part in one British yacht race, then make sure it's this one. The Round The Island Race is simply spectacular – and there is nothing so rewarding as a circumnavigation, even if it is only of the Isle of Wight.

The race is hosted by the Island Sailing Club in Cowes and was first sailed in 1931 with 25 entries doing battle for the Golden Roman Bowl, a copy of an actual archaeological find that had been dredged up from the Thames and caught the eye of the man who first conceived the race, Major Cyril Windeler.

The race was an annual event, and apart from the ban on private yachting during World War II, steadily grew over the decades with a record 1,875 entries in 2008. The event was first limited to small yachts but there is a more inclusive policy these days that welcomes everything from small open sports boats to Open 60 ocean racers and multihulls. The course starts from a line off the Island Sailing Club and takes the fleet clockwise around the Isle of Wight. The fastest time ever recorded for the 50.1m course was 3hr 8min, achieved by Francis Joyon on his trimaran *Idec* in 2001. Mike Slade, owner of the 100ft *Leopard,* holds the monohull record that he broke for a fourth time in 2008 and now stands at 3hr 53min. Some more modest cruising skippers are happy if they finish before nightfall.

With almost 2,000 yachts on the water, there is an element of survival to the race, especially because a large part of the fleet are cruising boats for whom this is a once a year foray into the world of racing. There are a few pitfalls that all skippers should do well to avoid, of which becoming ensnared in the Needles is perhaps the greatest. The rocky pillars of the Needles are the point where the fleet must close up before swinging around to the island's western shore. Some yachts try and cut the corner by passing between these chalk towers, a high-risk strategy known as 'threading the Needles'. The Needles become most congested in light winds and huge marine traffic jams have been known to form.

Cutting the corners can be tempting but each year many skippers are caught out by the ledges, shoals and sandbanks that litter the island's shore – and beware of following the boat in front as you never know how deep its keel is.

If you're serious about doing well, you'll read up about the shortcuts and snares in the books by local yachtsman Peter Bruce. If you follow his advice you'll also strip your boat of all extra gear before the start though dispensation is allowed for a bottle of grog with which to toast the completion of your race around the island.

category
boats

location
Caribbean

difficulty
tricky

time
all year

tempted by this?
try racing an Arabian dhow

ROLL A YOLE IN MARTINIQUE

Racing doesn't get more spectacular than onboard these colourful craft

The yoles of Martinique are the most colourful and exciting boats on the planet and racing upon one is an unforgettable experience. These 10.4-metre vessels are just 1.5 metres wide and fly enormous sails despite having no keel and carrying no stabilizing ballast.

That they remain upright at all is due to the efforts of their highly athletic crew and the long poles they use to balance these remarkable craft. More than half of the crew spend the races dashing from side to side and hanging from the 3.6-metre bamboo poles that extend over the water. Forget harnesses, trapezes and the wings that feature on modern skiffs, this is sailing at its simplest and most extreme.

With the poles wedged on the downwind side and sticking out to windward, the crews climb out to keep the yole on an even keel. Half a dozen crew must work together, shifting their weight constantly to counteract the gusts and squalls. Tacking is a thing of beauty as each crew member slips inboard, unhitches the pole, slides it across the boat and climbs out the other side as the bow passes through the wind.

These poles act as long levers, magnifying the righting moment of the crew and so allowing gigantic sails to be flown from vast spritsail rigs. There are classes for smaller yoles but the biggest, most popular class features craft with a small mast forward and a larger spar just behind. There is virtually no standing rigging and the masts are made of solid wood.

The yole is steered by a huge oar that extends from the stern and three crew are required to hold a steady course in the stiff Caribbean breeze. Capsizes are common and yet crews have a 'never say die' attitude: the boats are quickly righted and bailed out. Each yole comes from different village on the island and the competition is fierce. Brightly coloured sails are emblazoned with sponsors' logos and, along with luridly painted hulls, add to the vibrancy of the event.

There are regular Sunday races from March until December but the highlight of the calendar is a round-the-island event. During the end of July and early August the yoles race around the coast, stopping at seven villages over seven days and always drawing huge crowds.

These yoles are developments of the local fishing boats and their skippers and crews exhibit remarkable skill and strength as they blast through the blue seas of the Caribbean. Not only do they make a remarkable spectacle, they also show that you don't need carbon-fibre and Kevlar to go fast or have a lot of fun.

RALLY AROUND THE WORLD

Join a cruise in company on a global scale

Many yachtsmen and women have enough money to sail around but are short of time or concerned about safety. They start to plan a world-girdling cruise but soon come up against countless questions. What papers do you need to clear customs in Fiji and when's the best time to transit the Panama Canal? What jabs do you need for Mauritius and where do you get spares on the Galapagos Islands. The list is as long as the ocean is deep.

Fortunately there are several organizations that exist to help sailors circle the globe and help with many of the logistical problems along the way. Blue Water Rallies (BWR) helps 30 or more yachts sail around the world every two years. The BWR route is the one taken by the majority of European cruising yachts and sees the fleet set sail from Gibraltar in early autumn, stopping at the Canaries and Caribbean before passing through the Panama Canal. From there the Pacific lies ahead and crews visit the Galapagos Islands, as well as the far flung Marquesas, Tahiti, Tonga, Fiji and Mackay before reaching Darwin on the northern coast of Australia. Indonesia, Singapore, Thailand and Sri Lanka lie ahead before the homeward legs from Djibouti, through the Suez Canal and finally from Crete to Gibraltar.

The voyage takes some 20 months and a support crew is on hand to assist crews at 19 stops along the way. There are also extensive periods of 'free cruising' when skippers are encouraged to explore the local waters and set their own itinerary before meeting up to complete the next major leg in company.

World ARC is the other round-the-world rally and is run by the same company that organizes the Atlantic Rally for Cruisers (ARC), which helps a fleet of more than 200 cruising yachts sail from the Canaries to the Caribbean every year. St Lucia is the end of that event and the start of World ARC. From there the yachts follow a broadly similar route as the Blue Water Rally fleet through the Panama Canal and across the Pacific.

Australian landfall is made at Cairns and the yachts then head to Darwin and Indonesia before setting sail across the wide Indian Ocean to the tiny Cocos Islands and then onto Mauritius, Reunion and Richard's Bay, just north of Durban on the eastern coast of South Africa. Cape Town is the next port of call before the yachts head across the Atlantic via St Helena to explore Brazil and return to St Lucia via Trinidad.

Both events provide information and training prior to the start and both operate radio reporting schedules to allow yachts to stay in touch during the long ocean legs.

category
*voyages and
destinations*

location
Brittany, France

difficulty
moderate

time
all year

tempted by this?
*try sailing up the
Amazon*

RIDE THE TIDES IN
THE GOLFE DU MORBIHAN

The inland sea that is full of challenge
and delights

The Golfe du Morbihan lies on the coast of southern Brittany and is one of the most exciting inland waters that an adventurous sailor can sail. The Golfe is a huge basin, dotted with rocks and islands and covering an area of almost 129 square kilometres. What makes this area so exciting are the tides that rush in and out twice a day. The entrance to the Golfe is just 800 metres across and the larger islands further constrict – and so accelerate – the passage of water.

Currents can race at up to 9 knots, faster than most yachts can sail or motor, and there is often no option but to drop the anchor and wait for the foul tide to turn fair before continuing explorations of this small inland sea. These very strong tides create equally strong back eddies, where the rushing water swirls back onto itself. Careful navigation and plenty of local knowledge allows daring sailors to ride these currents and cheat the tide.

Of course, if the tide is heading where you want to go it will shoot you along with it, like enjoying a ride on a high-speed conveyor belt. Staying in control of your yacht in such extreme currents is a skill that needs to be mastered quickly because the buoys that mark the channels are unforgiving in a collision. Many of the channels are marked with leading lines: pairs of markers that, when lined up, tell the watchful skipper that the yacht is on the right course.

To add to the excitement there is a seaplane landing strip where anchoring is forbidden (for obvious reasons). Oyster beds present another hazard: the French love their oysters and the farming of these molluscs is a serious business with large human-made beds lying just beneath the swirling surface of the sea.

There are more than 40 islands, islets and rocks punctuating the Golfe. Some, like Ile aux Moines, are home to communities whereas others are only big enough for a single house or field.

Any would-be explorer of this fascinating cruising ground is well advised to track down a copy of 'Oyster River – One Summer on an Inland Sea'. This is a true-life adventure story written by George Millar, a hero of the Second World War. Millar explores the Golfe du Morbihan during an extended cruise and comes across some hidden sides of the area and those who sail and live there.

The joy of the area comes in exploring among these many islands – mastering the tides allows the exploration of many interesting coves and bays. The tourists may swarm around the main island villages during the summer but with a tide table and a strong nerve there are still many secret delights to discover.

EXPLORE THE CAPE VERDES

Venture off the beaten track
to lose your head in the clouds

Atlantic
Ocean

Mauritania

Cape Verdes

Dakar   Senegal

The Gambia

Guinea-Bissau

Lying some 600 km off the coast of Africa is a group of islands that could have been designed with the adventurous sailor in mind. The Cape Verde archipelago is made up of ten islands and eight smaller islets and offers challenging sailing and spectacular scenery in equal measure.

To enjoy the delights of these exceptional islands you first have to reach them. From mainland Europe this means a sail southwest, beyond Gibraltar and on past the Canaries. The Cape Verdes rise up from the Atlantic and are spread out over hundreds of kilometres in two groups. Santo Antão, São Vicente, Santa Luzia, São Nicolau, Sal and Boa Vista make up the Barlavento or windward islands, while the Sotavento or leeward islands are Maio, Santiago, Fogo and Brava.

It is the incredible cultural and geographic variety of the islands that make them so rewarding to visit. The Portuguese ruled from the 15th century until independence was granted in 1975. For centuries the islands were an important base for slavery and the proximity of the mainland means that there is a predominantly African feel with a touch of Portuguese, which can be detected in the culture and language, and especially the traditional morna music, a cross between the tango and the blues. Visitors describe a population that's poor but incredibly welcoming and generous.

Santo Antão is unmissable, but remember to pack your walking boots because you can discover its true beauty only by climbing across the interior . The island receives almost no rain but the condensation from the clouds that form around its volcanic peaks is enough to support lush vegetation and feed thundering waterfalls. Walking through the peaks and ravines of these cloud forests is an unforgettable experience and one that relatively few Western visitors have enjoyed.

The chain of islands runs southeast and includes the small yet stunning Santa Luzia and the striking São Nicolau with its mountains and beaches of black sand. Boa Vista, more than 160 km to the east, is a true desert island with sand dunes and desolation all around. Fogo to the south boasts the highest peak and an active volcano that is rich with sugar cane.

The waters between the islands are exposed to the Atlantic swell and the wind often blows at Force 4 or 5, and yet the climate hovers between 25°C and 29°C. There are few all-weather ports and at most of the islands the only option is to anchor off one of the many sandy beaches. Visiting these islands requires an adventurous spirit and this has kept them unspoilt. The idyllic climate is attracting tourism development and so would-be visitors shouldn't wait too long if they want to see the Cape Verdes in all their natural splendour.

Category
Experiences

Location
Arctic Circle

Difficulty
Tricky

Time
Autumn/Spring

Tempted by this?
*Why not explore
Antarctica?*

SAIL BENEATH THE NORTHERN LIGHTS

See the greatest light show on earth from the cockpit of your yacht

Venture far enough north, towards the magnetic pole, and you will eventually come across the Northern Lights or aurora borealis. This spectacular phenomenon illuminates the sky with a myriad magical colours and is one of the greatest natural wonders that can be seen from Earth.

Witnessing such a fantastic sight from the cockpit of a yacht makes the experience all the more special, especially as you will have had to overcome many nautical challenges to sail so far north.

The Northern Lights can be seen all round the world, but Norway makes an excellent base from which to start your celestial sailing adventure. You'll need to sail north, beyond the Arctic Circle, the line of latitude that runs at 66° 34" 03'. This is the point where the sun shines for 24 hours in the summer yet does not rise above the horizon for days on end during the winter.

The coast of north Norway may be part of the Land of the Midnight Sun but, thanks to the warming effect of the Gulf Stream, it does not experience the extreme low temperatures found at similar latitudes at other points of the globe. Sailing in Norway is as testing as it is rewarding: navigation is not for the faint hearted with numerous rock-strewn passages between steep sided islands. The coastline is largely uninhabited and sailors can truly get back to nature and enjoy a world untouched by man. The few fishing communities are small and populated by a race of people who have learnt to live near the ends of the earth. There are few sizeable cities and harbours along the way where natural resources including oil and gas have attracted workers and those who make a living from them. Tromsø is a perfect port to aim for, a teeming town at which to stock up on provisions before heading further north – and the home of the world's most northerly brewery. Heading further north there is a chance to drop anchor at Alta and see rock carvings that date from 4500BC as well as visiting Alta Canyon, the largest in Northern Europe. This is a place of extremes and if you call in to Hammerfest, make sure the log book shows that you have visited the world's most northernmost city.

Continuing towards the pole you will be rounding the North Cape, the extreme tip of Europe. Steep cliffs, wide bays and deep fjords create a stunning backdrop for adventurous yachtsmen who sail this far north. The mountains may be covered in snow and giant towers of ice may float through the water but this is a region that can be explored in everyday cruising yachts as sanctuary is never far away. The sun does not set here from May to July so if you want to see the Northern Lights you'll need to return in the autumn or spring.

RIDE THE ROLLER COASTER

The Newport-Bermuda race has a long history and a surprisingly challenging course

category
races and rallies

location
western Atlantic

difficulty
tricky

time
June

tempted by this?
try entering the South Atlantic Race

On paper it looks simple. Set sail from Newport, USA, and steer a course of 149° True for 1016 km; that's the rhumb line for the oldest of all offshore yachting events, the Newport-Bermuda Race.

The reality is a great deal more complicated. This is a true blue water race, with land only in sight for a few hours after the start and before the finish. The race is held every two years and around 180 yachts of all sizes take on the challenges of the Atlantic as they make their way to Bermuda, a speck in the vast ocean.

The greatest challenge comes as the yachts pass through the Gulf Stream. This immensely powerful ocean current causes large waves to form and can generate its own violent weather systems. The might of the Gulf Stream is almost impossible to comprehend: it is around 100 km wide and 100 metres deep, transports water at a rate of more than 100 million cubic metres per second and can run at more than 5 knots.

Picking the best spot to cross the Gulf Stream is essential to success in the Newport-Bermuda race; however, this is easier said than done because the current is constantly moving. Additional side currents and eddies flow from the main Gulf Stream and skilful or fortunate sailors can use these as high speed conveyor belts to pass swiftly through the fleet.

Modern technology allows modern sailors to pinpoint the position and movements of the Gulf Stream using satellite imagery – and so pick the perfect course through the worst of the breaking seas.

This mid-ocean roller-coaster ride is often followed by periods of lighter airs as the fleet approaches Bermuda. The race takes place in June and often starts in fog off Rhode Island, but is normally completed in baking sun and little breeze with exhausted sailors desperate to cross the finishing line. The final few kilometres can be the most challenging as navigators pick their way through the coral reefs that surround Bermuda.

The first race was organized in 1906 by Thomas Fleming Day, editor of *The Rudder* magazine. Day flew in the face of public opinion, which believed that only the largest sailing vessels were safe enough to cross open oceans. The initial race was a success and the event has maintained an enviable safety record for more than a century. The Newport-Bermuda Race has also moved with the times by introducing new classes to accommodate professional crews and super-maxis with canting keels. It is a pivotal part of the international racing calendar and credited with inspiring the creation of the Fastnet and Sydney-Hobart races.

Today the race is organized jointly by the Cruising Club of America and the Royal Bermudan Yacht Club. Some 45,000 sailors have competed, logging around 48 million kilometres between them.

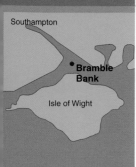

Southampton

● **Bramble Bank**

Isle of Wight

category
experiences

location
the Solent, UK

difficulty
simple

time
*a few hours, once
a year*

tempted by this?
*try a Caribbean cricket
cruise*

PLAY CRICKET IN THE MIDDLE OF THE SEA

Take part in one of the world's most unique sporting events

For 364 days of the year, the Bramble Bank is a hazard to shipping that sailors steer well clear of. However, for one day each summer, this sandbank that lies in the Solent between the Isle of Wight and Southampton, becomes the venue for an extraordinary sporting occasion.

The Bramble Bank Cricket Match is held annually between teams from the Royal Southern Yacht Club and the Island Sailing Club. Oilskins are swapped for cricket whites as the yachts sail towards the notorious shallows where many vessels, including the QE2, have gone aground. Anchors are dropped and the teams rush onto the sandbank as soon as the first sign of dry land appears.

The bank only dries at extremely low Spring tides and the sailors know that they will have only an hour or so to enjoy their sporting endeavours until the sea reclaims the pitch. Spectators watch from their own yachts and some venture ashore to sit at hastily erected picnic tables and enjoy a drink at the Bramble Inn, the 'pub' that only exists for minutes each year.

With stumps shoved into the wet sand, the umpires take their positions and play can commence. The boundary is marked by the lapping waves and players often stand with their feet just below the level of the sea, creating the eerie impression that they are walking on water, something that not even the great WG Grace could achieve. The pitch is neither flat nor true because the sand is not just rippled but contains sizeable puddles and pools.

Rules are not strictly enforced and scoring is a hit and miss affair, but no one minds because the result is a foregone conclusion – another exceptional feature of this match. The competing teams long ago decided that the sensible thing to do was to take turns to win and so the result is known before the first thud of sandy leather against salty willow.

After an hour and a half, the tide returns and the game is abandoned for another year as players and spectators scrabble to the yachts and motorboats that will take them back across some of the busiest waters in the world to a celebratory meal at the winner's club.

Cricket isn't the only game played on this narrow strip of sand. Two teams of children enjoyed a game of rugby in 2007 with the resulting sponsorship funds going, rather fittingly, to the Royal National Lifeboat Institute, whose crews are frequent visitors to the Bramble Bank when assisting yachts that have gone aground.

SAIL IN THE 'WORLD'S BEST HARBOUR'

Race or cruise past iconic Australian landmarks in Sydney Harbour

category
voyages and destinations

location
Australia

difficulty
simple

time
all year

tempted by this?
try sailing into Rio de Janeiro

It was an Englishman, Governor Arthur Phillip, who declared that while exploring the eastern coast of Australia he had 'the satisfaction of finding the finest harbour in the world, in which a thousand sail of the line may ride in the most perfect security'. Phillip went on to found the first colony but it was Lieutenant James Cook who initially discovered these protected waters, which he named Port Jackson after one of the Lord Commissioners of the British Admiralty, and Judge Advocate of the Fleet.

Port Jackson is the name still given to the waters, including Sydney Harbour itself, that lie to the west of an imaginary line between North and South Head at the mouth of what is actually a drowned river valley or ria. It is the harbour, however, and not the port that is famous worldwide, thanks in part to the iconic structures of the Sydney Harbour Bridge and Sydney Opera House. These triumphs of architecture and engineering are the cherry on the cake of an aquatic expanse that offers great sailing in the heart of a stunning, sun-soaked city.

The harbour is some 19 km long and covers an area of 52 square kilometres. The numerous inlets and bays create an expansive shoreline of 317 km and allow plenty of water frontage for the residents of Sydney, who generally live on the northern shore while the commercial activity takes place to the south.

With deep water, fresh winds and sunshine in plentiful supply it is inevitable that sailors will take to the water and there is a very active sailing scene around the harbour. Racing is organized throughout the year and there are classes to cater for everything from yachts of more than 20 metres to large fleets of Optimist dinghies sailed single-handedly by children.

The Cruising Yacht Club of Australia organizes many of the sailing events and its Monday night Spinnaker Races are a good combination of competition and fun. There is a large class of Sydney 38 one-design yachts that always provide tight racing and the 5.5-metre skiffs that first graced these waters in 1892 still compete, providing thrilling racing and spectacular wipe-outs.

There are plenty of charter boats available if you would like to explore Sydney Harbour at a more leisurely pace; you can choose whether to skipper the boat yourself or relax and soak up the scenery while someone else sails you through this spectacular sailing spot.

SAIL BACK INTO HISTORY

Follow the wake of our ancestors in historical craft

category
boats

location
Pacific/Atlantic

difficulty
extreme

time
57–101 days

tempted by this?
try sailing a Viking boat

Thor Heyerdahl is one of the greatest ocean adventurer of modern times. While some sailors were trying to set records for the speed or originality of their voyages, Heyerdahl was doing the exact opposite. He chose to retrace the sea voyages of ancient civilizations, not to earn a place in the history books but to rewrite them. His desire when setting sail was to test his theories about what craft could have crossed which waters and when. His were archaeological adventures that could not have been more challenging or dangerous and they went on to inspire future generations of academic explorers.

Heyerdahl's first love was zoology and as a student he lived and worked on the isolated island of Fatuhiva in the Marquesas group of Pacific islands. His interest was in the animal life but he soon became fascinated by how the islands' human inhabitants had first reached the islands. His theory suggested that the initial visitors had reached Polynesia via Peru and Easter Island on balsa rafts. This view was rejected by his fellow academics and so Heyerdahl set about putting his theory into practice.

In 1947 he constructed a 13.7-metre raft of 60-cm thick balsa logs that were lashed to crossbeams and covered by a bamboo deck. A bi-pod mast carried a square sail and a hut on the deck offered some protection from the sun. The vessel was named Kon-Tiki and during the course of 101 days sailed some 8,000 km over the Pacific Ocean before landing on the Raroia Atoll in the Tuamotu Archipelago.

Kon-Tiki was equipped with a steering oar but Heyerdahl discovered that direction could be more easily controlled by adjusting the position and depth of its five centreboards. These boards were so effective that the raft could be sailed at right angles to the wind, something that had previously been considered impossible.

The strength of the raft lay in her simplicity. The outside of the balsa wood logs became soft, preventing chafing of the ropes that held them together. The bamboo deck allowed water to drain away quickly, and the raft would just rise over the ocean swell, providing no resistance and so incurring no damage.

Conditions onboard Kon-Tiki were incredibly hard for Heyerdahl and his five crew. The experience didn't put him off ocean voyages in historic replicas though, and his work on Easter Island led him to investigate the capabilities of reed boats. In 1969 he set sail from Morocco bound for Barbados on board a large reed vessel, similar to those used by ancient Egyptians. Received wisdom was that these craft would only last a few weeks before the reeds rotted away.

The voyage had to be abandoned after covering 8,046 km, but Heyerdahl built a stronger craft, Ra II, and sailed this 12-metre craft some 6,100 km across the Atlantic in 57 days.

Heyerdahl went on to complete further epic voyages, each of them with the goal of a greater understanding of humans' past as well as highlighting the danger that pollution of the oceans was presenting for the future.

Cornwall

Land's End

category
voyages and destinations

location
southwest UK

difficulty
tricky

time
all year

tempted by this?
try sailing around Ardnamurchan

VENTURE AROUND LAND'S END

Sail past the rocks and reefs of England's most westerly point

Headlands fascinate sailors. They mark the dividing line between seas or oceans and are the turning points of passages, whether modest or epic. Land's End, the most westerly point of England, is one such turning point for yachts bound between the south coast and Ireland, Wales or the west coast. Forget to turn the corner at Land's End and you'll make landfall in America, because only open water lies between and nothing shelters Land's End from the might of Atlantic gales.

The headland is not just exposed; it's also surrounded by off-lying rocks on which numerous vessels have been wrecked. The Longships reef is the most notorious of these and is marked by an tall white lighthouse that flashes its warning to passing shipping. Local people who made their living from shipwrecks were less than impressed when Samuel Wyatt of Trinity House built the first Longships Light in 1794. That structure was replaced in 1873 by the lighthouse that still stands today. The men who used to tend the light have been replaced by automated machinery because they were frequently cut off for weeks at a time. The rocks around the reef are wonderfully named and skippers are well advised to steer clear of Kettle's Bottom, Shark's Fin and the Three Stone Oar rocks that lie beyond.

Commercial shipping passes to seaward of the Longships light, but yachts heading around the coast of Cornwall can pass inside, threading their way between the reef and Land's End. It is not a shortcut to be attempted in anything but calm conditions and only a lunatic would try it at night, but armed with a stout heart and a copy of the *West Country Cruising* pilot book, it should present few problems.

Mark Fishwick, author of that treasured tome, describes the area as 'a menacing stretch of water where you will probably feel little inclined to linger' and most sailors push on and put some distance between the fragile hull of their vessel and the cliffs that rise up to 70 metres above the chill sea.

Once clear of Land's End, there's little hope of nearby sanctuary. The coast of North Cornwall offers no safe harbour accessible in all weathers and most ports dry out completely. To the south, the fishing harbour at Newlyn is accessible at all states of tide but is not easy to enter in a swell. Many sailors continue towards Falmouth and so sail around the Lizard, thus passing England's extreme southerly and westerly points on the same passage.

GO FLY A KITE

Kitesurfing is the fastest form of sailing on the planet

category
boats

location
worldwide

difficulty
tricky

time
all year

tempted by this?
try wakeboarding behind a trimaran

Kitesurfing has turned the sailing world on its head. This most extreme of all nautical activities breaks almost every rule in the book – perhaps that's why it's so incredibly popular. Boats are meant to float, and yet kitesurfing boards sink the moment you stand on them. Traditional sailors rely on sails, masts, tillers and keels, yet kitesurfers put their faith in an air pump and a handlebar.

The disciplines are so different that some sailors deny that kitesurfing is sailing at all. Their refusal to welcome these newcomers into the fold may have something to do with jealousy. Kitesurfing has a lot going for it: the Holy Grail of sailing at 50 knots was achieved by a kitesurfer, the kit fits into a rucksack and is relatively inexpensive, and what other form of sailing allows you to take to the air and hang there for tens of seconds?

Kitesurfers have also earned themselves some bad press through a lack of consideration for other water users who may not be used to the speed with which these board riders skim across the sea. The greatest danger is from the kite strings, which have been known to slice ears off, though it is the riders themselves who are most at risk.

The kites have a surface area of 5–15 square metres and are flown from two, four or five lines of around 25 metres. These lines are connected to a control bar that is in turn linked to the kitesurfer's harness. Tilt the bar in the direction you want the kite to go and keep it level if you want it to go straight up and so depower. All control systems have a fail safe that collapses the kite if the rider loses control and lets go of the bar.

Boards are around 1.4 metres long and are shaped according to their principal use with disciplines including speed sailing, jumping, surf riding or upwind sailing. The majority of boards are symmetrical 'twin-tips' that allow either end to become the 'bow'.

The great breakthrough in the sport came with the invention of kites that could be re-launched from the water. This was possible by creating an inflatable tube along the leading edge of the kite that gave it buoyancy. Modern kites are generally very forgiving to fly and will stay airborne even if the rider ends up in the sea. In this case the person merely powers up the kite by steering it across the wind and pops out of the water just like water-skiers rise out of the water by angling their skis.

Once moving, the planing action keeps the kitesurfer afloat and then it's time to try some jumps as the rider accelerates the kite to create maximum power and lift. Once aloft he or she can attempt a dazzling array of acrobatics before landing and, hopefully, continuing this high-adrenalin adventure.

SAIL TO AFRICA

Discover a continent on your doorstep

category
voyages and destinations

location
Mediterranean

difficulty
moderate

time
all year

tempted by this?
try crossing the English Channel

Sailing to Africa conjures up images of explorations of the Congo and thoughts of the *Heart of Darkness*. That side of Africa does exist, and adventurous sailors will be welcomed up and down the coast of this great continent.

Senegal, for example, is a fascinating country to visit by yacht, particularly if you speak French, and a trip up the Saloum river south of Dakar is highly recommended. Stop at the village of Djifère before heading through the mangroves to enjoy cruising that's truly off the beaten track.

Senegal is only a small detour for yachts visiting the nearby Cape Verde islands, but for most European sailors it is far from their usual cruising grounds. Fortunately it is possible to sail to Africa and back in a day from British soil, well, from Gibraltar at least. Just 14.2 km separates mainland Europe from Morocco, meaning that you can sail to a new continent for lunch and be back in time for tea. From Gibraltar to the nearest African port is a passage of 24 km.

The Strait of Gibraltar is the gateway to the Mediterranean and presents a challenging passage to the cruising sailor. Those sailing from the virtually tideless waters of the Med will have to get used to the twice daily ebb and flow of the sea, whereas those approaching from the vast open waters of the Atlantic will need to adjust to the confined waters where shipping is funnelled through a marine motorway.

Of these two challenges, the commercial marine traffic is by far the most hazardous and skippers have to pick their gap carefully between the constant stream of east and west-going traffic. A night crossing can be easiest because navigation lights are harder to confuse than modern hull shapes, which are so various that it's impossible to tell the bows from the stern of many craft.

One set of vessels that will be carrying no lights at all are the cigarette boats that blast across these waters under the cover of darkness. These hugely powerful speedboats are used for smuggling and will sometimes flash past unwary yachts as they take their illicit cargo from coast to coast.

Ceuta is the nearest port on the African mainland, though it is actually an autonomous city of Spain and the possible site of one of the pillars of Hercules that once flanked the strait. For a more African feel, head south along the Moroccan coast to the small marina of Smir. The port itself is a rather lifeless place, but take a taxi inland to one of the walled towns and you feel yourself transported back a thousand years as you wander the souk and get lost among the maze of alleys. There are few places where a day's sail takes you to a different continent and a different millennia, but Gibraltar is one.

TAKE A SHORTCUT TO THE MEDITERRANEAN

Explore the heart of France and cut out the Bay of Biscay

Crossing the Bay of Biscay is an undoubtedly adventurous undertaking and essential if you wish to sail from the UK to the Mediterranean. There is, however, another way to take your yacht south to the sun while enjoying a very different type of adventure.

Crossing France from north to south via rivers and canals presents sailors with a view of the country that they may never otherwise see. Not only does it avoid a possibly hazardous sea passage across open stretches of the Atlantic, it also allows the exploration the French interior from the comfort of one's own boat.

The principal cross-country route is from Le Havre, along the Seine and the Yonne rivers before picking up the canal network that will transport you to the mighty Rhone. Having crossed the Channel the first job is to have the mast lowered because the minimum clearance beneath bridges is 3.5 metres. Some skippers choose to carry their mast lying flat along the deck and construct special struts to support it. Others pay to have the spar transported by lorry to the Mediterranean coast, rather than spend weeks banging their head or tripping over bits of rigging. Expect to pay over €1000 for this service.

With the mast lowered, you can now focus on protecting your yacht's fragile hull from the concrete lock walls that you'll be encountering time and again before reaching Homer's 'wine dark sea'. Car tyres are the solution to fendering problems and there is normally a pile of them by the crane that lowers your mast. These tyres are left by yachts that have transited from the other direction and so are constantly shifted from coast to coast. The tyres may stop your sides being scratched but will leave black marks all over your hull, and so wrap them in bin bags or keep them away from your hull by hanging your own fenders, then a horizontal plank and then the tyres.

For this journey you'll need the right paperwork, and with ever changing regulations you're advised to check with the Royal Yachting Association on the latest requirements before you set off. As well as a height limit, your craft needs to have a keel no deeper than 1.8 metres and a maximum width of 5 metres.

If you can satisfy these criteria, you're ready to head south for over 1,600 km, with more than 100 locks between you and the sea. One of the first highlights is to pass through the heart of Paris, and Arles and Avignon are worthwhile detours towards the end of the journey. Some people complete the coast to coast trip in a fortnight whereas others spend years enjoying the delights of this gentle inland adventure.

category
experience

location
worldwide

difficulty
tricky

time
all year

tempted?
try climbing the mast at sea

SPINNAKER SWING

Let the wind take you higher

There's always one more job to do onboard a yacht. Ropes to splice, decks to swab or hatches to batten down. There does, however, come a time on every boat when the crew just wants to play and it's a brave skipper who denies their wish.

Swimming is the most obvious leisure pursuit if the sun is out and the water warm. The yacht provides a perfect diving platform and there will soon be bodies leaping from stem to stern. Eventually the swimmers will start to look for more adventurous aquatic options and this is where the spinnaker swing comes in.

To start, the boat must be anchored from the stern so that its bow is pointing away from the wind. The spinnaker, a giant colourful sail that is used to power yachts downwind, is then hoisted to the top of the mast as usual but instead of its corners, or clews, being secured to the boat, they are attached to one another with a long loop or rope. As the wind fills the sail, the halyard that holds it to the top of the mast is slowly let out until the spinnaker is flying above open water.

It is now that the adventurous crew member sits in (or clings on to) the loop of rope and is lifted skyward as the sail fills. If you're feeling fancy, use a plank or bosun's chair to create a proper seat – though the ability to make a quick escape is crucial.

With the crew member in the loop, it is just a question of waiting for the wind to fill the sail. As the colourful canvas billows, it lifts the person out of the water and the swimmer becomes a swinger. The harder the wind blows, the higher the crew goes. If it all becomes a little scary the quick solution is to let go of the rope or slip from the swing and plunge into the water below. Those on the boat can also control the height of the swing by paying out more rope from the top of the mast. Extra lines led from the clews of the sail to the boat can also control the height of swing but will make the yacht start to sail.

Swinging beneath a spinnaker is an incredible sensation and is spectacular to watch. The forces exerted on the mast and rigging are similar to those experienced when flying the spinnaker conventionally, so next time the sun is out and the crew look bored, why not give it a try.

CHARTER THE MALTESE FALCON

You need a big wallet but a small crew to enjoy this sailing sensation

No other vessel on the planet is as distinctive, technologically advanced or downright awe-inspiring as the Maltese Falcon. She's a staggering 88 metres long and 12.6 metres wide, but what sets apart is her unique rig.

Masts are normally supported by wires – but not on this work of engineering genius. The three 58.2-metre spars are made of carbon fibre and totally unsupported. A series of yard-arms extend from each mast, reminiscent of a traditional square-rigged ship. There's nothing traditional about the Maltese Falcon, however, and her 15 sails are unfurled at a touch of the button, taking six minutes to deploy fully. Each mast can be rotated to stand at the perfect angle at the wind and the sails join up with those above and below to create one vast expanse of canvas.

This DynaRig arrangement was first dreamt up in the 1960s as a way to use the wind to help power commercial ships across the world's oceans. The idea never took off but when Tom Perkins, owner of the Maltese Falcon, was searching for innovative ways to power his new yacht he invested in the research and production facilities to turn the theory into practice. The sails are controlled by a computer system that monitors wind speed and direction and the skipper sits at a space age console, adjusting the 2,400 square metres of sail at the touch of a button.

With the deck free of ropes and rigging, there is more than enough space for the 12 guests to relax on one of the three decks. The guests are outnumbered by crew, with the captain supported by a crew of engineers, a chef and a team of hostesses to ensure that passengers want for nothing. There is a personal trainer on board to put guests through their paces in the onboard gym or give them a sports massage just in case they pull a muscle reaching for the suntan lotion.

There are plenty of toys for those who want to make a splash. As well as two 9.7-metre RIBs, there are four Laser dinghies, a jet-powered tender, six sets of diving gear and plenty of water-skis and wakeboards. One of the latest additions to the Maltese Falcon's armoury of amusement is the 'deep flight' submarine, which is used to allow guests to explore the world beneath the waves. Instead of ballast tanks the sub is able to dive by flying through the water and angling small wings downwards to descend to around 122 metres.

Such luxuries do not come cheap and Maltese Falcon costs US$350,000 a week to charter. It's a huge amount of money, although the thrill of blasting through the waves at up to 20 knots on the most remarkable sailing boat ever built may just qualify as a priceless experience.

Brazil

Rio de
Janeiro

SAIL IN THE SHADOW OF THE SUGAR LOAF

Rio de Janeiro is an exotic ocean crossroads

Visiting the River of January may not sound too appealing, but translate the phrase into Portuguese and images of one of the most iconic harbours in the world spring to mind. Rio de Janeiro is not just a city in a spectacular setting, it is also a major port of call for yachtsmen and women sailing the world's oceans. Such places where the excitement of making a landfall combine with dramatic backdrops earn ports such as Rio, Cape Town and San Francisco a special place in sailors' hearts.

Two recognizable sights strike seafarers as this famous Brazilian city appears over the horizon: the statue of Christ the Redeemer that stands on Corcovado Hill, 710 metres above sea level, and lower down at 396 metres, but just as unmistakable, Sugar Loaf Mountain – spot these two sites and you know that your passage is almost over.

These landmarks have lifted the spirits of the hundreds of competitive sailors who have cruised into Rio with the fleets of numerous round-the-world events including the Volvo Ocean Race, BT Global Challenge and BOC Challenge. Some of these sailors will be heading southwards, and will party hard before setting off to face the gales and icebergs of the Southern Ocean. Others have left the terrors of the Roaring Forties behind them and may be looking forward to setting a course that carries them north and homewards. Whichever way they are bound, you can bet that they would have enjoyed some Rio 'R and R' with a cold beer on Copacabana beach while watching the girls in bikinis for whom the Brazilian was invented.

For other sailors, Rio is the finish line: the Cape to Rio Race was a non-stop 5760-km sprint across the Southern Atlantic from Cape Town and was the high point of the South African sailing calendar. It has been renamed the South Atlantic Race and now varies its end point, alternating Rio with Punta del Este in Uruguay and Salvador in Brazil.

Sailors have always included Rio de Janeiro on their passage plans when sailing the coast of South America. There are several marinas and anchorages conveniently located to explore the city that was founded by the Portuguese in the 16th century and was Brazil's capital until 1960. The Iate Clube do Rio de Janeiro is the heart of the sailing scene and plays host to all the major yachting events. If the hustle and bustle of the city gets too much, up-anchor and move across Guanabara Bay to the quieter community of Niterói. Time your cruise to arrive in Rio in February and you'll be able to enjoy the world famous carnival without having to pay inflated hotel room prices.

FRYING FLYING FISH

Enjoy the sailor's breakfast that delivers itself

category
experiences

location
*tropical and
subtropical waters*

difficulty
simple

time
all year

tempted by this?
try eating sushi at sea

There are many things that can only be experienced at sea but none are quite as peculiar as eating a breakfast that's delivered to your door even though you're hundreds of kilometres from land. Flying fish regularly land on the deck of a yacht – and those that don't tumble back over the side make a tasty meal. These crash landings normally happen at night when the fish can't see where they're going and in the warm waters where they are most likely to be found it makes sense to eat them when they're fresh. So it is that flying fish are regularly served for breakfast on yachts the world over.

The phenomena of flying fish is something that needs to be seen to be believed with fish reaching heights of over a metre and having been recorded spending up to 45 seconds airborne.

These plankton eaters live close to the surface and take to the air to avoid predators such as swordfish and tuna. They fire themselves out of the water with a flick of their tail fin and then extend their wing-like pectoral fins to glide over the waves. Some also have large rear pelvic fins giving the effect of two pairs of wings. Their eyes are specially adapted to see above the water and they can follow the crests of waves, riding the updraft, or change course to stream downwind, away from their attackers. By flicking their tail they can gain extra speed allowing them to skim across the water. An average glide is 30–50 metres in length.

There are more than 50 species of flying fish and they are found in all the major oceans, particularly in the warm tropical and subtropical waters of the Atlantic, Pacific and Indian oceans. The Greek name for these remarkable creatures is Exocoetidae, which in turn led to the naming of the Exocet anti-ship missile that can be launched from submarines.

It's all too easy for flying fish to end up on deck as the leeward or downwind side of a yacht is often just centimetres from the water and in strong winds the edge of the boat may be awash for long periods. The sails also act as giant nets to catch the unlucky fish whose flight path coincides with the yacht's course. Most fish will have knocked themselves out or suffocated out of water; if they are still alive a blow to the back of the head with a winch handle will ensure a quick dispatch. Sizes vary, but 30 centimetres is good and 45 centimetres exceptional. De-scale your fish and then cut off the head, fins and slit the belly open to remove the guts. In the Far East, the roe or *tobiko* of the Japanese flying fish is prized by sushi connoisseurs and is sometimes used as an ingredient in California rolls.

Most sailors favour a quick flash in a pan with a knob of butter. Jack London, that great adventurer of the early 19th century enjoyed them that way and declared that 'flying-fish are most toothsome for breakfast'.

RACE A TRANSPAC

The TP52 circuit is yacht racing at its glamorous best

category
boats

location
Mediterranean

difficulty
tricky

time
April–October

tempted by this?
try racing a Volvo 70

The America's Cup may be the pinnacle of the sport of 'round the cans' sailing but it is an irregular event that often becomes bogged down in its own complex rules. Things are more straightforward in the world of the Transpac 52 (TP52), in which simplicity and speed make for some of the tightest, most exciting big boat racing on the water.

The TP52 class was formed in 2001 and grew first in America before becoming the premiere class in Europe. This move across the Atlantic was accelerated when King Juan Carlos of Spain decided to join the circuit and gave it added credibility and appeal.

All TP52 yachts are built to a 'box rule', which states that the vessels should fit in a theoretical box of certain dimensions. Length, displacement, draft and sail area are strictly controlled whereas hull shape, keel shape, construction, interiors, deck layout and rigging are virtually unregulated. Crew weight is limited to 1270 kg, which equates to about 14 sailors. Complicated systems such as water ballast, canting keels and running back stays were excluded to ensure safe and reliable boats that can sail offshore as well as around inshore courses.

The yachts may have similar dimensions but this is no one-design class where all the boats are identical. The rules allow for constant design innovation and the use of carbon fibre and other high-tech materials. This is seriously big budget boating and only the richest teams stand a chance of winning. Competition is fierce and huge sums are spent on hiring the best professional sailors and ensuring boats are in pristine condition. There is no handicapping and so the first boat over the line is always the winner. A class for amateur crews does encourage those with smaller budgets to join the ever growing fleet.

The TP52 is a class for extremely fast boats and speeds of over 25 knots are recorded when sailing downwind. Around 60 percent of each yacht's weight is in the keel, allowing them to drive upwind under full sail with the crew dangling over the windward side to keep the boat more upright and so fractionally faster.

The focus of the TP52 calendar is the MedCup with six events around the Mediterranean in which more than 20 yachts compete, making it the leading Grand Prix sailing event. In excess of 50 TP52s have been built, though some are optimized for handicap racing in other parts of the world.

Sailing a TP52 is an unbelievable thrill. Lightweight construction, a heavy keel and a wide flat hull make up a supercharged yacht that handles more like a dinghy. With little to go wrong, the crews can push to the limit and close, thrilling racing is guaranteed.

SURVIVE
IN A LIFERAFT

Could you cope with 117 days adrift?

How do you like your seagull: medium rare or well done? It's not a question most people have to ask themselves but if you find yourself adrift in a liferaft with little chance of rescue, eating seagulls could be all that keeps you alive.

The most important thing to remember about abandoning ship and taking to the liferafts is that it is an absolute last resort. Sailors joke that one should only step up into a liferaft (as your yacht sinks beneath you), but the point is a serious one. Even a swamped or listing yacht is a safer refuge than a lifeboat and is far easier for the rescue services to detect.

If the worst happens and you do have to inflate your liferaft, make sure that it's tied on securely before you throw it over the side.

You can't be sure how long you'll be adrift and having adequate water is the key to your survival. If there is time, fill jerry cans with spare drinking water, leaving good-sized air gaps to ensure they float. Take whatever you can that will prolong your life and aid your rescue. A handheld VHF radio, emergency beacon, spare batteries, flares, foghorn, binoculars, first aid kit and a small mirror for signalling will all help get you noticed. A CD makes an adequate substitute for a mirror and be less likely to smash. As well as water you should take food, clothing and a first aid kit. Even the best sailors can suffer from debilitating seasickness once in a liferaft and that in turn causes dehydration, and so anti-sickness pills are a must.

If you were able to broadcast a Mayday message before leaving your vessel and you know that it was received, the emergency pack that is contained within the liferaft should have enough to keep you going if help is on its way. If lightening destroyed your electronics and set fire to your boat, think about taking extra fishing gear.

One cruising couple, Maurice and Maralyn Bailey, spent almost four months floating about the Pacific in a liferaft after their yacht sank. In their book, *117 Days Adrift,* they describe their life or death adventure and how they survived on a diet of seagull, turtle and rainwater.

If your yacht is about to sink it may be sensible to take to the liferaft but remain tied on the mother ship, thus making a larger target for the search and rescue team. Keep a sharp knife to hand to cut the rope should the yacht start to go down, but do be careful not to puncture your new craft.

category
races and rallies

location
Irish Sea

difficulty
extreme

time
June

tempted by this?
try racing around the Baltic

CONQUER THE THREE PEAKS

The truly adventurous event where mountain running and sailing combine

The Three Peaks Yacht Race is not for the faint-hearted. Indeed it is not advised for any but the best sailors and fittest athletes, because it combines sailing along some of Britain's least hospitable coastline with running up the three highest mountains of England, Scotland and Wales.

The event starts in the Welsh port of Barmouth and sees yachts with crews of five set sail northwards to Caernarfon where they put two runners ashore. These athletes have to summit Snowdon, 1,085 metres above sea level, and return to their vessel before it can cast off for Whitehaven. This passage takes yachts through the notorious Menai Straits and beyond where fast tides, oil rigs and large ships combine to create plenty of navigational hazards.

The next port of call is Whitehaven where the runners must again hit the shore at speed for ahead of them towers Scafell Pike, the highest mountain in England at 978 metres. The distance from the coast to the foot of the mountain is significant and so runners cycle the 24 km or more from Whitehaven to Gillerthwaite before starting their ascent. Bicycles may be carried on the boat or support teams may have them waiting ashore.

On their return to Whitehaven, there is another testing sea crossing to Fort William on the western coast of Scotland. The greatest challenge of the event is still to be faced because the final summit is that of Ben Nevis, 1,344 metres above sea level, which is of course where the runners must start from. The clock is finally stopped when both runners return to the landing point.

The race involves 622 km of sailing, 48 km in the saddle and 115 km of running or walking. Conditions can be extremely dangerous near the summits and competitors may have to deal with snow and ice. The legs-on-land involve a total ascent of 4,267 metres.

The race is open to monohull yachts and engine power can only be used close to port, although yachts can be rowed or paddled. There are no handicaps or time adjustments: it's a straight race and the first team to get their runners back to their yacht in Fort William, having climbed all the mountains, wins the coveted Daily Telegraph Cup.

category
experiences

location
Brittany, France

difficulty
simple

time
every four years

tempted by this?
*try sailing aboard a
tall ship*

BREST IS BEST

Everyone is welcome at the Brest Maritime Festival

Sail to the French port of Brest during its week-long sailing festival and experience a celebration of all things nautical that cannot be matched for size, splendour or sheer joie de vivre.

The Brest Maritime Festival is held every four years and the 2008 festival saw almost 2,000 vessels sail to the harbour on the north-western tip of Brittany to take part in the fun. It's an open church with every sort of craft from historic replicas to the latest ocean racers.

There are coasters, fishing boats and working boats, classic boats, small traditional craft and skiffs, classic motorboats from the 'belle epoque', exotic boats such as Asian junks, pirogues and boats from the West Indies, the Southern Ocean and Polynesia. Famous record breakers tie up alongside crab boats and everyone enjoys the excitement. Rowing boats and open boats share the water and dockside with elegant tall ships whose crew line the yard-arms, dozens of metres above well scrubbed decks.

The latest event was a United Nations of the sea with crews and craft from France, Spain, Holland, Germany, Ireland, Norway, Denmark, Vietnam, Switzerland, Croatia, USA, Madagascar, Russia, Australia, Brazil, Japan, New Zealand and the UK. Over the years there have been jangadas, twangas, junks and dragon boats among the mix of traditional craft from across the globe.

There's plenty to see ashore and some 500,000 visitors visit the festival. An international village shows off the boat building, craft and culinary skills of a wide range of countries and there's always live music and plenty of fruit de mer. Indeed, the festival is used as a showcase for the best of Brittany and you can learn about anything from rabbit production to oyster dredging.

The first Brest Maritime Festival took place in 1992 and saw such legends of the sea as Eric Tabarly and Robin Knox-Johnston sail to the event that became an instant success. Traditional and historic vessels are at the heart of the action and many replicas and restorations make their debuts at Brest.

The fleet is split into three equal groups, with a third of the boats setting sail for a short cruise, a third manoeuvring within the harbour and the remaining vessels staying tied up in the marina. The spectacle continues on dry land with a street theatre troupe, live music and the odd sea shanty too. It all goes to make for a uniquely colourful way to celebrate the sea and the ships that sail upon it.

WINDSURF ACROSS AN OCEAN

You need a big board and plenty of guts

Sailing across an ocean onboard a yacht is enough for most sailors. The more adventurous may sail solo, or in a small or open boat. Only the bravest and most adventurous would set sail across open water on a windsurfer, but that's exactly what a middle-aged Frenchwoman has done repeatedly.

Raphaëla le Gouvello is one of the world's great adventurers and a national hero. Her extreme windsurfing career started in 2000 when, aged 40, she sailed a windsurfer across the Atlantic. This remarkable feat had been done before, by Frenchman Stephane Peyron in 1987, and Raphaëla used his board to replicate the achievement.

This was no ordinary windsurf board that can be carried in one hand. This was a 7.5-metre monster that was 1.3 metres wide and contained several watertight compartments, the largest of which was big enough for Raphaëla to sleep in during her crossing from Dakar, Senegal to Guadeloupe. The 5093km crossing took 58 days and the lightly-built yachtswoman spent 361 hours sailing the board with no automated systems to help her.

Raphaëla had to take down the mast and de-rig the sail each night before stowing them securely and locking herself in her coffin-like cabin. She lay there at the mercy of the wind and the waves until the morning when she would have to balance in the Atlantic swell and try and re-rig the 6.6-square-metre sail without losing the rig or herself overboard.

She survived the challenge and etched her name in the record books but wasn't satisfied. Two years later she took on the more modest challenge of sailing across the Mediterranean from Marseilles to Tunisia, a feat she accomplished in 10 days having battled headwinds, busy shipping lanes and currents that drove her backwards at night. The Med crossing, however, was merely an appetizer for her next challenge in 2003: to cross the Pacific from Peru to Tahiti. This mind-boggling 12,874-km passage took a staggering 89 days and involved long periods of seasickness in the ocean swell of these shark-infested waters. Raphaëla would sail for around seven hours each day, having to eat every few hours to maintain her strength and constantly fighting painful shoulders and elbows caused by holding the tall rig upright. This did not stop her from pushing hard when conditions were right and she recorded speeds of over 8 knots.

This quietly-spoken sailor still hadn't had enough and took on the Indian Ocean in 2006, sailing from north-west Australia to Reunion Island, a 5249-km crossing that took 60 days and supposedly marked the end of Raphaëla's ocean adventures.

She continues to sail though, and in 2007 completed a 724-km tour of Brittany, visiting 26 ports and spreading her message of sustainable development and ecological awareness. Raphaëla is a great environmental ambassador because few people can claim a closer relationship with the world's oceans.

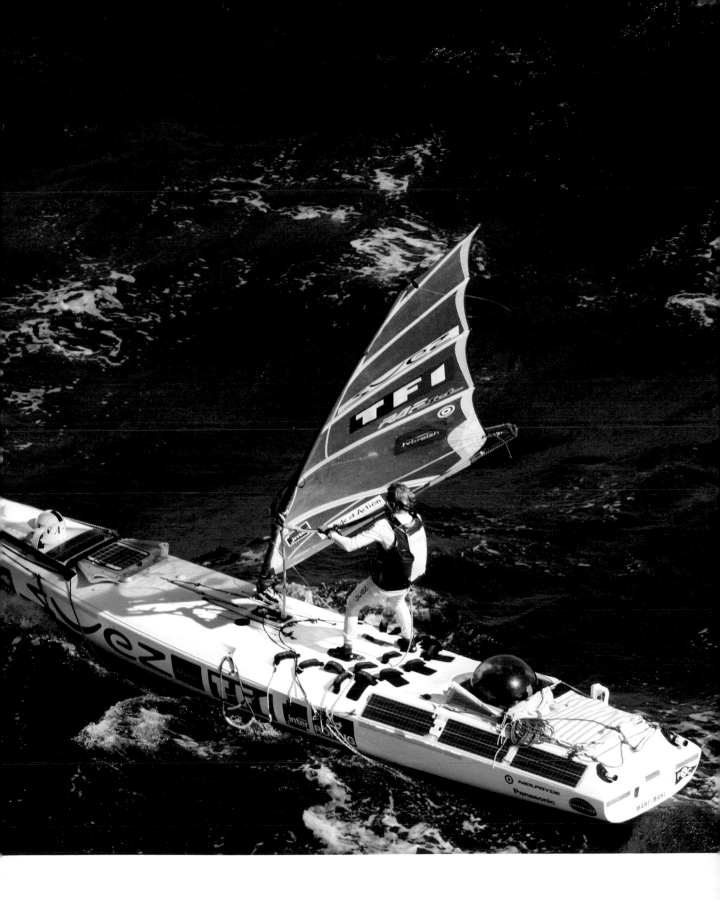

WRESTLE WITH A BIG CAT

Have the ride of your life on maxi-cat

category
boats

location
worldwide

difficulty
extreme

time
all year

tempted by this?
*try entering the
Vendée Globe*

Maxi-catamarans are built with just one goal: to race across oceans as fast as possible. These incredible sailing machines have shrunk the globe and allowed lightening quick circumnavigations. Maxi-cats such as Playstati on, Club Med and Orange II were designed to shatter records and they succeeded.

In 1994, the record for 'distance sailed in a day' stood at 864 km and was held by Primagaz, a 20-metre trimaran. The advent of the maxi-cats saw that figure rise to 1225 km by 2006 when, onboard Orange II, Bruno Peyron maintained an average speed of 31.95 knots for 24 hours.

Such speeds were made possible by the sheer scale of these giant catamarans. Playstation (now known as Cheyenne) is 38 metres long and 35.8 metres wide. Her mast stands 45 metres tall and she has a downwind sail area of 3,546 square metres.

Most of the maxi-cats were created to compete in The Race, a no-limits, non-stop, round-the-world sprint that started in Barcelona at the dawn of the new millennium in 2000. Large catamarans already existed and had set world records, but nothing had been built on the scale of these ocean leviathans.

Not all the designs were successful. The most daring was that of Team Philips, the twin-masted cat skippered by Pete Goss. The boat was fast but simply not strong enough to resist the battering she received from an Atlantic storm during pre-race sea trials. The futuristic craft broke apart, leaving more traditional competitors to race around the globe.

There has, however, not been another event on the scale of The Race and the limelight has turned away from maxi-cats to trimarans and singlehanded record attempts. In 2007, onboard Groupama 3, a 32-metre tri, Franck Cammas covered 1270 km in 24 hours at an average of 33 knots. It's an incredible feat and shows the potential of these three-hulled racing machines.

The round-the-world record is still held by a maxi-cat, however. Orange II circled the globe in a breathtaking 50 days back in 2005 and it will take a special boat, a remarkable crew and perfect weather to beat that remarkable record.

The statistics may be impressive but they give no idea of what life is like onboard a maxi-cat as it races across the water. The twin hulls of a catamaran have a very different motion to the relatively predictable movement of a monohull. Crewing a maxi-cat is like riding a bucking bronco strapped to a rollercoaster, going through a carwash in a storm. Huge mesh trampolines stretch between the two hulls and the team onboard have to cling on for their lives as massive waves smash across the boat. Capsize is a constant danger and catamarans do not right themselves as monohulls do.

Add the freezing waters, massive waves and icebergs of the Southern Ocean and it is clear why the men and women who race these vessels are among the most adventurous of all those who set sail.

category
voyages and destinations

location
London, UK

difficulty
moderate

time
all year

tempted by this?
try sailing into Cape Town

SAIL UP THE THAMES

Stop the traffic in the heart of London

Modern London is a cosmopolitan city that's served by five international airports – but it was once a thriving port. The River Thames was the lifeblood of the capital and ships came from all over the world to load and unload their cargos.

These were the days before auxiliary engines and skippers had to use the tides to carry their heavily laden craft upstream. With the current against them there was little choice but to throw out the anchor and wait for the foul tide to turn fair.

These were also the days of the Thames barges, great gaff-rigged vessels that plied their trade up and down the river and in the estuaries around it. Vessels of 24 metres or more were crewed by a man and a boy who would have to take them through the narrow entrances of docks and alongside wharfs under sail alone.

Thames barges still sail this ancient river though cargos of wheat and coal have been replaced by charter customers and classic boat enthusiasts. The river itself has also changed, most significantly with the addition of the Thames Barrier that protects the city from flooding. The barrier stretches 520 metres from bank to bank at Woolwich Reach, some 8 km east of Tower Bridge. Construction of the barrier finished in 1983 and the design includes four 61-metre spans for shipping to pass through.

Sailing through the barrier at the end of a long sea passage is a thrilling experience. Behind you are the shifting sands of the East Coast that have claimed so many vessels bound for London. The wind turbines that now stand off the mouth of the Thames Estuary will have disappeared astern and you have already slipped beneath the towering Dartford Bridge.

With luck you'll have a rare easterly wind to blow you towards the glinting glass and steel of Canary Wharf's skyscrapers and the regenerated business and residential areas that lie around them. Docklands is the new financial hub of the capital but was once the heart of its marine activity with the wharfs lined with shipping from the far-flung empire.

Look to port as you pass round the Isle of Dogs and you'll see Greenwich, the home of the Prime Meridian, that vital reference point that helped sailors explore the world's oceans and allowed them to find their way home again.

Follow the twists of the river, passing Rotherhithe and Surrey Docks, and there before you with the Tower of London on the north bank and HMS Belfast standing sentinel to the south is Tower Bridge. This iconic river crossing was opened in 1894 and the bascules have been raising to allow shipping to pass beneath ever since. Clearance below is 8.6 metres when closed and 42.5 metres when open. The bascules are raised around 1,000 times a year and river traffic still takes priority over road traffic, although 24 hours' notice is required before opening the bridge.

To pass under the bridge under sail is an unforgettable experience and announces the end of your city sailing exploits, because passing any farther upstream requires masts to be dropped before passing under the 104 bridges that lie ahead.

SAIL AROUND BRITAIN

Circumnavigating the busy shores of mainland Britain is one of the toughest sailing challenges

category
races and rallies

location
UK

difficulty
tough

time
four days +

tempted by this?
try sailing around Ireland

What are the greatest challenges and hazards that face the skipper of a yacht? Strong tides are tricky, rocks are never fun and commercial shipping is always a danger. All three of these hazards are plentiful around the coast of mainland Great Britain and account for the fact that more sailors cross the Atlantic each year than circumnavigate the island that they call home.

Measuring the exact length of the United Kingdom coastline is an almost impossible task because of the countless inlets, crags and outcrops, though a figure of around 12,300 km is generally accepted. That total includes all the UK's islands, of which there are more than 1,000. A sailor clearly doesn't need to hug the coast or sail around each island and so faces something nearer a 4,000-km voyage around this sceptred isle.

The biggest decision a prospective circumnavigator must face is whether to turn to port or starboard on first leaving harbour. With prevailing winds from the southwest, it is generally considered wise to put the wheel to port and attempt an anti-clockwise voyage. This should allow you to complete the long stretches of Britain's south and east coasts with the wind helping you along. Heading down the Irish Sea into the breeze is likely to be problematic, although careful observation of approaching weather fronts should allow opportunities to sail with the wind abaft the beam (more with you than against you).

Next you must decide how often you will be stopping on your adventure. Calling into port every night adds many hundreds of kilometres to the journey and may be impossible in some parts of the country, especially if your yacht is not able to dry out and remain upright. A combination of long passages and short hops is a sensible solution, allowing skippers to bypass unwelcoming coasts and linger over the safer more scenic spots.

The final crucial choice is whether to take a short cut across Scotland and miss out on hundreds of kilometres of sailing through the roughest, most exposed seas around the British Isles. Many supposed circumnavigations of the UK pass through the Caledonian Canal that connects the Scottish west coast at Corpach near Fort William with the east coast at Inverness. This 100-km route through lochs and canals bypasses the northern tip of Scotland and the Orkneys and isles of Skye and Lewis. For those short of time or nerve it is a sensible option but means that no claims can be made to have truly 'sailed around Britain'.

The most adventurous may wish to attempt a non-stop circumnavigation. The catamaran Playstation sailed around Britain and Ireland in 4 days, 16 hours, and the monohull record stands at 7 days, 4 hours.

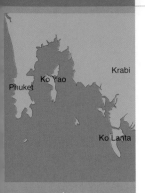

category
voyages and destinations

location
Thailand

difficulty
simple

time
all year

tempted by this?
try sailing a Gunboat

GO BACK TO NATURE IN THAILAND

Let it all hang out on an eco-charter in the Andaman Sea

You can't get much closer to nature than on the deck of a yacht, surrounded by crystal clear waters. Add breathtaking limestone islands, draped in thick vegetation, and you have a snapshot of sailing in Thailand's Andaman Sea.

When visiting somewhere so natural and beautiful it makes sense to do so in a vessel that's sympathetic to the surroundings, and nothing fits the bill as well as a Tiki catamaran. These simple, twin-hulled craft are modelled on the boats that allowed the Polynesians to explore the wide, open waters of the Pacific. They are low-tech and all the more attractive for it, though in recent years a number of well-appointed examples have been built in Thailand specifically for the charter market.

There are many reasons why a catamaran is this perfect craft in which to explore these waters. The wide decks are ideal places for lying under the sun or stretching out in the shade. Catamarans have very shallow hulls and so can be sailed right up onto the beach or taken to areas too shallow for normal yachts. There are extensive shallows in the north of the Andaman Sea and a cat will take you to stunning parts of this nature reserve where there is virtually no development and the only shopping you will be able to buy is from passing fishing boats.

Tiki catamarans were first created by James Wharram, a British yacht designer who proved their seaworthiness by sailing one across the Atlantic. He went on to design bigger and bigger boats and Wharram Cats, as they are also known, have sailed to most corners of the globe. Wharram sold the plans to his boats and thousands of people bought them, in the hope of building their own catamarans and escaping to distant horizons. Wharram himself embraced the simple life and he and his crew were well known for sailing in the nude whenever possible. Many Tiki sailors follow his example, leaving their inhibitions on dry land.

Of course naked navigation isn't essential when chartering a Tiki catamaran in Thailand. Indeed, if you opt for the more luxurious and fully-crewed 16.7-metre versions, it's probably discouraged. There is however a certain appeal to turning your back on all the trappings of modern life and, whether naked or not, exploring these tranquil waters while leaving behind the smallest carbon footprint possible.

ACCEPT THE JESTER CHALLENGE

Sail across the Atlantic the old fashioned way

category
races and rallies

location
north Atlantic

difficulty
tough

time
weeks or months

tempted by this?
*try crossing an ocean
in a micro cruiser*

Sailing can be a dangerous sport and every year brings new pronouncements that dictate what equipment yachts should carry before racing offshore. Extra kit may boost safety but it also increases cost, sometimes to the point that eager competitors have to exclude themselves on financial grounds.

Flying in the face of this rule-setting and expense is the Jester Challenge, a transatlantic race that believes small is beautiful and that responsibility lies with the individual. It's a view shared by many yachtsmen and women who pine for the simpler sailing of yesteryear when all that was needed was a small boat and a star to steer her by. The race is run every four years, starting from Plymouth, UK, and finishing in Newport, Rhode Island, USA. The number of entrants is growing with each event and although many will not make it to the start line and fewer still make it across the Atlantic, the Corinthian spirit is clearly still alive and well in ocean yacht racing.

The event is named after the yacht Jester, a 7.6-metre Folkboat that was adapted with a fully enclosed cockpit and junk rig. She was dreamed up by Blondie Haslar as a craft that could be sailed through all weathers without exposing the solo skipper to the dangers of being on deck. The sail and steering can be controlled from inside the boat or from a small hatch.

It was Haslar who came up with the idea of a single-handed yacht race from the UK to America, against the prevailing winds. The first race, organized by the Royal Western Yacht Club and sponsored by *The Observer* newspaper, was held in 1960 from Plymouth to New York and won by Francis Chichester in Gipsy Moth II; Jester came second. The race has been held every four years since 1960 and there has been a Jester in each one though the original boat was lost at sea and replaced by a replica.

The Observer Single-handed Transatlantic Race (OSTAR) paved the way for the ocean races that followed but the entry requirements became increasingly difficult for the owners of small yachts to adhere to. When the minimum length for the OSTAR was set at 10 metres Jester was excluded, though still welcomed as an honoured guest. This move led to the creation of the Jester Challenge, a transatlantic race with no entry fees, no inspections and no regulations dictating safety equipment. Responsibility lies squarely with the skipper and although only two of the ten boats finished the inaugural 2006 event, none of the fleet required outside assistance, despite atrocious conditions.

The Jester Challenge allows like-minded skippers to race across an ocean in the humblest of craft with no safety net. Only the truly adventurous need apply.

CROSS THE EQUATOR

Pay homage to Neptune as you sail between hemispheres

Are you a shellback or a pollywog? If you're not sure you're almost certainly the latter, because the rite of passage to become the former is something you are unlikely to forget. A shellback is someone who has crossed the equator by boat and the occasion is marked by an anarchic ceremony that dates back many hundreds of years.

Overseeing the line-crossing rituals is Lord Neptune, a member of the crew who has crossed the equator before and who stands proud with a trident, crown and flowing robes. Neptune appears at all ceremonies but the rest of the details vary from navy to navy as well as from yacht to yacht.

Some crossing-the-line ceremonies used to involve severe physical abuse and it was only towards the end of the 20th century that navies laid down rules to limit the excesses of the crew. Yachtsmen and women have never been quite so extreme, but humiliation and mess is all part of the fun and modern day pollywogs can expect to become covered in all sorts of slime and muck before the day is out.

First, the pollywogs must be 'prepared' to meet Neptune. This can involve any range of tricky tests and unpleasant activities from eating foul-tasting or oddly-coloured food to kissing the stomach of the Royal Baby. The baby is another crewmember (often the fattest), dressed in a nappy, and with all sorts of foulness from chilli sauce to axle grease smeared on the belly. Other 'royal officers' may also conduct fake preparations, all of which involve a degree of mess and humiliation.

Before the pollywogs can be presented they must first be cleaned, though the water in which they are doused or dunked is often dyed an unappealing colour. Now, finally ready, they are led before Neptune who holds court, often accompanied by Queen Amphitrite and Davy Jones.

Neptune was the Roman god of the water but later became associated with his Greek equivalent, Poseidon. Davy Jones has a mysterious past and his character may have originated from the biblical tale of Jonah or be named after an English seaman who fell overboard. Some believe he was a pirate whose ship sank while crossing the equator. For the purposes of the ceremony, Davy Jones should be dressed in rags and either acts as a secretary to Neptune, ticking off the names of those who are about to become shellbacks, or take on the role of court jester. Triton, a merman son of Amphitrite and Poseidon, is also known to show his watery face from time to time.

In the court of King Neptune experience is all and sailors of any rank or standing must bow down before him if they are to join the ranks of the shellbacks that have 'crossed the line'.

WHEN BIG IS VERY BEAUTIFUL

J Class yachts epitomize the glory of sail

category
boats

location
worldwide

difficulty
moderate

time
all year

tempted by this?
try racing in the modern day America's Cup

J Class yachts stir something deep within every sailor's soul. The combination of power and elegance is utterly bewitching and the sight of one of these vessels under sail can never be forgotten. To helm one of the Js is to be a king of the yachting world, with dozens of courtiers trimming sheets and wrestling with vast expanses of canvas.

The first J Class yachts were built in 1930 and the design rule that brought them into existence was actually meant to promote more modest, affordable yachts. It is hard to believe, but these craft of up to 27 metres were small in comparison to the craft that had gone before them, such as the 45-metre Britannia that was built for King Edward VII when Prince of Wales in 1893 – and scuttled in 1936, as directed in his will. These relatively smaller, cheaper craft were built under the International Rule that allowed yachts of different sizes and design to race against each other. A vessel's various dimensions were fed through a formula and the resulting figure was the yacht's 'length' under the rule. J Class yachts all had a comparable rating length and were the largest craft ever built under the International Rule.

Ten J Class yachts were built between 1929 and 1937, and all but one competed in the America's Cup, the pinnacle of international yacht racing that had started in 1851. Enterprise, Whirlwind, Yankee, Weetamoe and Rainbow did battle for the Americans whereas Ranger, Shamrock V, Endeavour, Endeavour II and Velsheda represented Great Britain. The racing was tight but the Americans always retained the title due to a combination of brilliant design and sailing, deep pockets, luck and home advantage. The Stateside boats may have crossed the line first but it is the British boats that have triumphed against time. All of the American boats were scrapped in the late 1930s and 1940s, whereas three original British boats are still sailing.

The glorious sight of these classics under sail has whetted the appetite of those whose resources are as great as their passion for the sea. Reproduction Js such as Ranger are already competing in events in Europe and the Caribbean and more yachts are being built. As well as the recreation of yachts that were sailed then scrapped (all original J Class yachts were built of steel), there are several yachts that were designed but never built: vessels such as Svea, which were conceived in 1937 and is due to be launched, finally, in 2011.

It is the combination of a rich history, breathtaking beauty and stunning speed that has ensured that the J Class can look forwards to a sparkling future. The owners who pay for these yachts to be built, restored and maintained also look to cover their costs and many of the Js are available to charter, although if you need to ask how much, you simply can't afford it.

SAIL INTO THE DEPTHS OF DESOLATION

The waters of the north-eastern Pacific offer spectacular sailing

When Captain George Vancouver visited the waters that lie beyond the modern day city that bears his name, he reported that 'there was not a single prospect that was pleasing to the eye'. So it was that Desolation Sound was given its rather depressing name.

Times and tastes change, however, and the waters of Desolation Sound are now regarded as exceptionally beautiful. The inlets, bays and rivers of this unspoilt corner of British Columbia are undoubtedly a paradise for yachts.

The beauty of the area has been officially recognized and these waters form part of Desolation Sound Provincial Marine Park. There is a wealth of flora and fauna; killer whales and colonies of seals are common sights and the snow-capped mountains act as a backdrop to the granite fringed shore. Wild salmon return to these waters in late July before heading upstream to spawn in the higher reaches of the river. This is a great time to watch grizzly bears hunting along the shore and the deck of a yacht is the perfect place to watch this wealth of natural activity because bears don't like sailing!

Visitors can witness salmon leaping out of the water to escape the seals that are feasting on them. Mink are often seen, and beneath the waves are oysters in their thousands. A word of warning about these tempting molluscs: Desolation Sound is subject to occasional red tides, a bloom of microscopic marine organisms, which when concentrated in shellfish, can cause PSP (paralytic shellfish poisoning).

The Sound is home to the steepest drop from mountain peak to sea bottom in all of North America. Glacial waters feed thundering waterfalls but the temperature of the Sound itself reaches acceptable swimming temperatures in the summer. If the desolate name is putting you off, take comfort on the fact that these waters form part of the more optimistically named Sunshine Coast.

Desolation Sound is more than 258 km long but narrow, with around 30 km of open water between its shores. It has an incredible number of coves, rivers and bays, meaning that you could spend many weeks or months exploring it. The area is popular with boaters from nearby Vancouver and numerous charter companies offer yachts for charter. A two-week charter is recommended to allow enough time to explore such wonderfully named spots as Secret Cove, Blind Bay, Squirrel Cove and Harmony Islands – though be careful, names can be misleading!

GO ALOFT UNDER SAIL

Climb to the top of the towering mast

category
experience

location
worldwide

difficulty
moderate

time
minutes

tempted by this?
try spinnaker swinging

There are two ways to fix a problem at the top of the mast: take the mast down or climb up it. Lowering a mast is a complicated and expensive procedure and so trips to the masthead become an inevitable part of sailing, especially offshore when there is simply no alternative.

Masts act as giant levers, exaggerating the movement of the yacht below. A faint rocking at deck level is translated into a much more violent swaying at the top of the mast. No wonder that sailors prefer to climb the mast of a boat that's securely tied up in a marina. Of course it's not always possible to make a pit stop, especially on a round-the-world race, and in such cases there is no alternative but to make the ascent at sea. The first trick of going aloft at sea is to keep the sails up. It sounds odd to non-sailors, but the force of the wind on the sails actually steadies the boat. It may be heeled over but it's not bobbing around on the ocean swell as it would be if under bare poles.

To climb the mast you need a harness or bosun's chair to support your weight. On a fully crewed boat with big winches and plenty of muscle the climber just has to sit and enjoy the ride. On solo voyages, skippers must haul themselves up. Some offshore yachts are equipped with small footholds on the mast to make climbing easier; others carry special climbing kit that allows sailors to push themselves up using the strength of their legs. Many yachts are equipped with powered anchor windlasses and these should not be overlooked as a quick and easy way to go aloft.

The skippers of Open 60 yachts are very accustomed to mast-climbing during their solo ocean races, but this doesn't make the task any more enjoyable. Preparation is all important because they don't want to climb a 27-metre mast only to discover that they've taken the wrong sized spanner.

Tools should be attached to ropes that are tied to the harness and there should be a back up system to allow you to get down in case your harness jams. Skippers wear crash helmets as they are often thrown around when at the masthead: bruises are inevitable but concussion could be fatal. Indeed, some skippers tie themselves to the mast to stop them being swung into mid-air above the ocean that is shooting past so far beneath them. On a fine day – and with a strong crew to pull you up – there is an amazing sense of being on top of the world when suspended at the top of the mast of a yacht under sail.

Look out from the masthead of a yacht under sail in mid-ocean and you really feel like you're on top of the world.

India

Sri Lanka

Indian Ocean

Maldives
●

SURF SAFARI IN THE MALDIVES

Sail from break to break among these paradise islands

For some yachtsmen and women, sailing is an end in itself. Bernard Moitessier, a pioneering explorer, racer and marine mystic, chose not to cross the finishing line of the first ever round-the-world race. He was so happy at sea that he just kept going, following the horizon that remained forever distant.

Other sailors see their yachts as a means to end. They are the vehicles that allow them to reach places that are often inaccessible by those who must travel by land. Divers count among this number and so do surfers. There is a small band of yachtsmen and women who buck the trend and head towards the breaking waves. Surf and sailing make uneasy bedfellows but there are certain places where the two can happily coexist. The idyllic archipelago of the Maldives is one such location.

The 26 atolls that make up the Maldives are formed from 1,192 islets and islands, of which some 250 are inhabited. The land rises up almost vertically from the depths of the Indian Ocean and there are numerous spots where the combination of swell and reef combine to create some enticing breaks.

Which of these waves will be 'working' on any given day depends on the direction of the wind and the weather of the preceding days. Far off ocean storms may create beautiful breakers under the calmest of skies.

Some breaks are more reliable than others but the best way to find the surf is by boat. Once the perfect patch has been found, the skipper can sail close by and allow the surfers to jump off with their boards and paddle to the waves. There are few spots where yachts can be safely anchored while waves are ridden and so there is usually one poor soul who must hold the boat in position while his or her companions surf some of the most stunning seas on the planet.

In some instances another non-surfer in an inflatable dinghy will need to act as a taxi, ferrying the wave riders between break and boat.

Catamarans and shoal-draught yachts with shallow keels are best for exploring the reefs of the Maldives, but some round-the-world cruising yachts call at these paradise islands before heading up India's western coast towards the Red Sea and Suez Canal.

If taking your yacht to the Maldives presents some logistical difficulties, you can opt for one of the numerous local boats that take surfers on weeklong safaris among the surf.

THE FASTNET RACE

Blast round the rock in this offshore classic

category
races and rallies

location
Southern England

difficulty
moderate

time
August, every other year

tempted by this?
try the Sydney-Hobart Race

The Fastnet Race is one of the best-known sailing events in the world with a colourful history that involves both tragedy and triumph. The race starts off the Royal Yacht Squadron in Cowes on the Isle of Wight and the course leads west towards the open waters of the Atlantic, passing Anvil Point, Portland Bill, Start Point, The Lizard and Lands End. The turning point is Fastnet Rock itself, a tiny craggy island off the southern coast of Ireland. A tall lighthouse marks the rock, and once the fleet have rounded this iconic beacon the crews head for the finish line in Plymouth.

The 978-km race takes place straight after Cowes Week and many of the crews look forward to escaping the confines and close quarter manoeuvres of the Solent for the open waters of the English Channel.

The 1979 Fastnet Race became internationally infamous when the fleet was caught out in a massive depression in the Western Approaches where the English Channel opens up into the Atlantic. Of the 303 yachts that started the race, 23 were abandoned or sunk. Of the 2,500 sailors who took part, 136 were rescued; 15 people died. The tragedy was the result of freak weather coupled with a trend in yacht design for speed rather than safety.

The event is run by the Royal Ocean Racing Club and all participants must now complete 483 km of offshore racing before the event. There are also strict rules detailing what safety equipment must be carried.

The fleet is wonderfully mixed with some of the biggest, fastest yachts in the world taking part alongside small amateur crews. Many sailing schools and charter companies enter boats and offer Fastnet Race packages that ensure participants have logged the necessary kilometres and know what will be expected from them during the gruelling event. The fastest yachts are totally devoid of creature comforts and the extreme skippers require crew to spend every spare moment sitting 'on the rail' on the windward, wave-lashed side of the boat.

Leopard, a 30-metre supermaxi, set the course record at a staggering 1 day, 20 hours in 2007, although more modest yachts can expect to take around five days. Conditions are usually mixed with summer gales making appearances. It is also not uncommon for yachts to have to anchor to stop themselves drifting backwards if becalmed with the tide against them. It's all part of the variety that makes the Fastnet such a popular and challenging event.

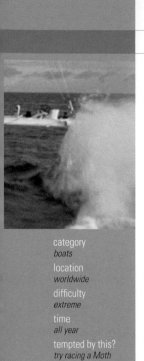

SET A WORLD SPEED RECORD

There are plenty of ways to become the fastest sailor on earth

category
boats

location
worldwide

difficulty
extreme

time
all year

tempted by this?
try racing a Moth

Sailors love to go fast and the more adventurous the sailor, the greater their need for speed. Some take this desire to the extreme and focus all their energies on becoming the fastest on the planet. Speed sailing is a surprisingly dynamic and diverse area of the sport where three very different approaches result in very similar speeds.

The first speed sailing record noted by the World Sailing Speed Record Council was set at 26.3 knots in 1972 by Tim Colman aboard his catamaran, Crossbow, on the waters off Portland, UK. Colman then spent a decade pushing his average speed over 500 metres, the official distance, up to 36 knots. That record stood until 1986 when a windsurfer reached 38.86 knots. The era of windsurfing record breakers continued and speeds slowly climbed until Frenchman Thierry Bielak reached 44.66 knots in 1991.

In 1993, an Australian boat named Yellow Pages Endeavour (YPE) became world famous when it set a new record of 46.52 knots. What earned YPE all this attention was not so much the speed as the boat's extraordinary design. This remarkable craft was built purely to sail fast over 500 metres and needed perfect conditions with flat water and not too much, not too little wind. A solid sail rested on a Y-shaped hull that could skim across the water but would virtually self-destruct if anything went wrong.

YPE's record did not last for long and windsurfers ruled supreme from 2004 until 2008, nudging the record to 49.09 knots, tantalizingly close to the Holy Grail of 50 knots. In fact it was a kitesurfer, Sebastien Cattelan, who beat the 50-knot barrier in the waters of Luderitz, Namibia, in 2008. Luderitz is the venue for regular international speed sailing events because it offers strong, steady winds and flat, shallow waters.

While the kitesurfers and windsurfers were blasting up and down the shore of Luderitz, another team of would-be record breakers were busy at work a few hundred kilometres north at Walvis Bay. The Vesta Sailrocket is an L-shaped craft with a 9-metre hull and a solid sail. It is designed so that the harder the wind blows, the faster the boat sails, with none of the problems of being overpowered and capsizing that limit normal sailing boats. Speeds of over 47 knots show that the theory works in practice but several highly dramatic and equally destructive crashes also demonstrate that tiny problems become disasters at high speed.

On the other side of the world in Australia, another purpose-built record breaker is also hovering around the 50-knot mark. Macquarie Innovation is the creation of the YPE designers and is built for winds of around 17 knots.

An entirely different approach is taken by l'Hydroptère, an 18.3-metre ocean-going trimaran that lifts out of the sea on foils. This remarkable vessel is skippered by Alain Thébault and has reached speeds of over 50 knots but not been able to sustain them over the 500-metre record course.

At the time of writing, both l'Hydroptère and Vesta Sailrocket are lying in pieces after high-speed capsizes while Macquarie Innovation's claim of a 50.7 knot measured-run is still to be confirmed. Meanwhile the 100 kilometres per hour record (54 knots) still beckons the bravest and fastest sailors in the world.

South Africa

Atlantic
Ocean

Indian
Ocean

**Cape of
Good Hope**

category
*voyages and
destinations*

location
southern Africa

difficulty
tricky

time
all year

tempted by this?
*try becoming a Cape
Horner*

ROUND THE CAPE OF GOOD HOPE

Sail around this mighty headland and discover Cape Town beyond

When it comes to boasting rights, the Cape of Good Hope can only be trumped by Cape Horn. The two great capes lie at the southern edges of the continents of Africa and South America and mark the entrance to the Atlantic Ocean. Or do they?

There is a popular misconception that the Cape of Good Hope is the most southerly point of Africa, but that honour goes to Cape Agulhas, some 160 km to the southeast. The Cape of Good Hope earned this reputation because it is the point at which yachts sailing down the western coast of Africa can finally make their course more easterly than southerly and start heading for the riches of the East Indies beyond. It is a spectacular headland, a narrow ridge of rock reaching out into the cold clear waters where the Atlantic and Pacific oceans meet.

Sailors passing the Cape of Good Hope are likely to be filled with strong emotions. If heading west, they are likely to have just experienced the thrill (or terror) or riding the mighty Agulhas current that sweeps down the coast of Africa and can produce waves that snap the largest ships in two. They may be battered and bruised but they know that around the famous headland are the many delights of Cape Town. Landfall here is a glorious thing and approaching Table Mountain and the city that lies beneath by boat is an unforgettable experience.

Cape Town has always welcomed seafarers and been able to supply the fresh food and drink for which they long. For modern sailor that means a visit to the Royal Cape Town Yacht Club, where stories can be shared and cold beer drunk before a visit to one of the countless restaurants offering stunning wines and wonderful food. After weeks at sea and the odd storm, it is truly paradise found.

The crews of yachts rounding the cape from west to east will be leaving Cape Town behind them. They'll be well rested but know that ahead of them lies the wide expanses of the Indian Ocean or the challenges of South Africa's rocky coastline where the surf is constant and ports of refuge are few and far between.

Skippers of non-stop, round-the-world races don't even have the pleasure of stopping at Cape Town before rounding the cape and heading towards the almost constant storms and icebergs of the Southern Ocean.

SUSHI AT SEA

Enjoy the freshest possible fish

Fish come from the sea. Yachts sail on the sea. Put the two together and you have the potential for a meal that's as delicious as it is free – and there's no simpler way to eat fish than as sushi, or, more accurately, sashimi.

There are a few obstacles to overcome, however, before you can sit down to enjoy your sophisticated fish dinner. The greatest of these is the actual catching of the fish and the trick here is to reduce speed. Skippers hate going slow but if you want a decent chance of securing your supper, you have to do so. If the log is showing more than 4 knots you'll be looking at SPAM for supper rather than sushi.

Your target fish will largely depend on the waters in which you're sailing. If cruising around the UK, why not set your sights on mackerel? It is not only the easiest fish to catch, it's also at its most delicious when eaten raw. A medium length line armed with shiny steel spinners is all you need. These little metal propellers spin around, catching the light and tempting the mackerel to bite. Brightly coloured feathers can prove an effective alternative and are also worth trying.

If you're ocean sailing, why not be ambitious and try to catch a tuna? You'll need a proper rod and some thick line or you're likely to lose the fish or the reel before you can land it. Tuna can be very large and no one wants to waste fish or spend hours wrestling with a monster of the deep when you should be sailing. The trick is to choose a small lure but arm it with a big hook. Visit the angling store and find something resembling a small, psychedelic squid. Then buy a hook 50 percent larger than the one that comes with the squid and you're ready to go. The idea is that the small lure will be ignored by the largest fish while the big hook is more likely to stop fish that do bite from getting away.

Once the fish has been caught and brought on board you'll need to kill it. A blow to the back of the head with a winch handle is the traditional method of dispatch, though sashimi literally means 'pierced body' and some believe that sashimi fish should be killed with a sharp spike passed through the brain.

Clean and gut the fish as quickly as possible and expect to get blood and scales everywhere. Cut away the fillets (tuna skin peels off remarkably easily before the fillet or loin has been cut away, whereas mackerel should be filleted and then de-skinned with a sharp knife).

Cut the raw fish into pieces about 2.5 cm wide, 4 cm long and 0.5 cm thick. Serve with soy sauce mixed with a little wasabi paste and thinly sliced pickled ginger. English mustard or horseradish and cucumber make an excellent alternative, especially to mackerel sashimi.

EXPLORE THE MYSTERIOUS EAST

Go on a voyage of discovery with the Eastern Mediterranean Yacht Rally

The Mediterranean is an idyllic cruising ground but many sailors limit their exploration to its northern shore. More adventurous yachtsmen and women may want to sail the eastern and southern coasts but are put off by political uncertainty, safety issues or problems with bureaucracy. Fortunately, an event exists that allows these open minded sailors to broaden their horizons on a rally that starts in Istanbul, Turkey, and finishes in Herzliya in Israel.

The Eastern Mediterranean Yacht Rally, also known as EMYR or the East Med Rally, stops at 21 ports in six countries and lasts for 75 days. It's a demanding schedule that sees yachts sailing by night and taking in the sights and sounds of each new port by day. There are organized tours, many of them lasting two days, as well as plenty of welcome parties and receptions organized by the host harbours.

The first month of the rally sees the fleet of up to 80 yachts cruise the coast of Turkey in 11 legs that cover over 1100 km. Turkish facilities are generally good and this part of the rally serves as a gentle introduction to the more demanding sailing and simpler facilities that are found on some of the 'international' legs.

The flotilla then stops at 11 harbours in Cyprus, Syria, Lebanon, Israel and Egypt and covers almost another 1600 km over 48 days. Crews can visit Damascus, Beirut and cruise the Nile (though not on their own boats). There are opportunities to visit 12 UNESCO World Heritage Sites and the route stops at ports in Europe, Asia and Africa. Sailors can leave their yachts to wander through mountain villages or try their hand at bartering in one of the many colourful markets.

The East Med Rally has taken place every year since 1990 and participants generally finish elated but exhausted. It's certainly a whistle stop tour that can only hope to give a flavour of the region, but it does serve to introduce sailors to an area that they may otherwise overlook completely. The organizers also hope that it will open the eyes of officials at the ports and harbours along the coast of the Eastern Mediterranean to the potential and possibilities that improved yachting facilities may bring.

Sailors from all nationalities take part in the rally and the attitude is one of tolerance and international cooperation. The organizers take the safety of participants very seriously and Coastguard escorts accompany the yachts on some legs. It is a remarkable event for adventurous sailors who wish to discover colourful countries with fascinating histories.

SAIL LIKE A VIKING

Cross the North Sea in search of black gold

The Vikings are widely recognized as some of the greatest seafarers of all time and are credited with making long ocean voyages in open boats. The only true way to discover how these warriors (and peaceful settlers) handled the challenges of navigation, tides, rough weather and provisioning is to recreate a Viking voyage – and that's exactly what a team of hardy historians have done.

Before attempting a Viking voyage you need a Viking boat. Fortunately the remains of a 30-metre vessel were discovered in Denmark. Skuldelev 2 is one of the largest and most sophisticated crafts ever discovered from this period and archaeologists pieced together her remains and used this information to create a replica. They also analysed the timbers and discovered that she had been built in around 1042 in Dublin, Ireland, a city that was founded by Viking settlers. If she had been sailed from Dublin to Denmark, her replica could be sailed back.

Four years of painstaking construction using traditional tools and techniques led to the construction of Sea Stallion. Over 7,000 iron nails and rivets, 2 km of rope and 300 oak trees were needed for its reconstruction. Next came the task of choosing the 65 volunteer crew, about the same number that would have sailed on the original Skuldelev 2.

With kit and food stored onboard, Sea Stallion set sail from Denmark on 1 July, 2007, bound for Dublin, 1,609 km away.

The journey that followed was a tale of hardship and headwinds with unseasonable summer gales testing the boat and crew to the limit. The ancient design proved itself incredibly capable and with the wind blowing from astern the single-sailed craft could reach speeds of up to 12 knots. The simple square of canvas did not perform so well with a headwind and it took a great deal of trial and error to find the best way to beat into the breeze.

What the crew dreaded most of all were calms because this meant rowing the vast and incredibly heavy craft. Sea Stallion carried 60 oars but only half of these would be used at one time, allowing rowers to rest between their backbreaking labours at the rowlocks.

The route took the boat and crew from Denmark to Norway and then across to the Orkneys at the tip of Scotland. Constant adverse weather forced the skipper to accept a tow across the North Sea – time was running out and the scheduled arrival time in Dublin could not be missed. It was a decision that saddened all onboard and leaves the door of opportunity open to other adventurers who fancy recreating the voyage unaided.

Sea Stallion continued through the Scottish islands and via the Isle of Man to Dublin. She received a very warm welcome with the crew enjoying the odd pint of celebratory Guinness, the black gold that had yet to be invented in the 11th century.

The crew had endured many sleepless nights on board with waves repeatedly breaking over those off-watch sailors who tried to grab some rest on the open deck. The six-week journey had not been without outside assistance but had proved that such boats were capable of crossing seas and delivering crew safely to shore.

RACE AROUND THE WORLD

Go from zero to hero with the Clipper Race

Taking part in a round-the-world yacht race seems beyond the realms of possibility for most mere mortals. Surely you need to be highly experienced with thousands of kilometres in your log book and numerous contacts in the racing fraternity to expect an invitation to join the crew of a round-the-world racing yacht.

That's certainly true for the professional races such as the Volvo Ocean Race but there is another option that allows anyone to set sail, whatever their experience. The Clipper Round the World Yacht Race caters specifically for those with little or no experience of offshore racing and gives a chance for the person in the street to realize the ambition of a lifetime. Ten identical yachts, each with a professional skipper and 17 amateur crew, sail some 56,000 km around the world in ten months. The circumnavigation is broken down into 14 separate races and the boats stop at five continents with time allowed for crews to explore countries such as Brazil, China, Australia and South Africa, depending on the length of the stopover.

As well as adequate physical ability, potential crew need to be able to get on with the others onboard and write a cheque for £32,000 for the full circumnavigation. It's a huge sum of money but does cover full training prior to the race as well as bed and board on the yacht for the 300-plus days you'll be away. Individual legs can be booked with crew flying out to meet the fleet and these cost around £4,000 each.

Crews vary in age and experience and every boat develops a different attitude and ethos to the event. Some are all about winning and all comforts are sacrificed to the god of speed. Others find the challenge of being at the competitive coal face for weeks on end a harder struggle, and thoughts turn to the social attractions when the race arrives in port. Which yacht will play which role is hard to predict and it is only when the racing starts that the true colours of the crews are shown during the hardships of night watches and gale-whipped sail changes.

The 21-metre yachts were designed specifically for the race and conditions for the crew are Spartan with simple bunks and zero privacy. There is no automated steering and sails have to be changed manually – a task that can involve going onto the foredeck in wild conditions as the bows bury beneath the foaming sea.

It's all character-building stuff and allows people from all walks of life to experience one of the great adventures that the sea has to offer.

SEE LIGHTS IN THE NIGHT

Marvel at an underwater light show

category
experience

location
worldwide

difficulty
simple

time
all year

tempted by this?
try marvelling at the Northern Lights

'A father and son were sailing in the Gulf of Mexico, far from shore, when their yacht capsized. As they clung to the upturned hull they saw two large, shimmering circles of light form around their boat. These rings of light went round and round, one within the other. In time they realized that the outer circle was made up of sharks, eager to attack, while the inner circle was created by dolphins, constantly blocking the way and keeping the sailors safe.'

Although this story is apocryphal, the reference to sea creatures creating trails of light is entirely accurate and watching a marine light show is one of the many rewards of sailing at night.

It is not just the bodies of dolphins and sharks that set the sea afire with blue-green light. Any disturbance of the water is enough to start the sea shimmering, though the cause of this wonderful phenomenon is less romantic than the effect it produces.

The dolphin's tail and the wake of a yacht glows because of the presence of blooming phytoplankton, especially the dinoflagellate *Noctiluca miliaris*. These microscopic creatures turn the energy of movement into light and coat the body of a swimmer with an eerie glow. They will also, somewhat alarmingly, illuminate the toilet bowl of a yacht when flushed with phosphorescent seawater.

Such phosphorescence turns a dolphin into a torpedo of light and there are few things as thrilling as being joined by one or more dolphins while standing a lonely night watch at the helm. They flash through the water, apparently just keeping up with the yacht, and then suddenly accelerate away, disappearing into the deep black darkness and leaving the ocean adventurer with an undeniable sense of awe.

Flashes of luminescence can also be caused by the numerous sea creatures that create their own light shows to attract prey, stay within schools or warn off predators. For example, many species of squid can emit luminous clouds when threatened.

Mariners report seeing other lights in the water whose cause is harder to explain. There are many documented accounts of strange patterns of luminescence coming from the depths. The Royal Netherlands Meteorological Institute has researched sightings of marine phosphorescent wheels that circle ships with rings and spokes of light. Scientists cannot agree whether these are caused by waves acting as lenses or by shockwaves caused by seaquakes. Metal ships sailing into areas where there were anomalies in the earth's geomagnetic field has also been suggested as causing these wheels and balls of light, though the jury is still out. What is certain is that the sea still contains many mysteries and those who sail upon it are constantly venturing into the unknown.

English Channel

Brest

Bay
of
Biscay

Santander

category
*voyages and
destinations*

location
eastern Atlantic

difficulty
tricky

time
all year

tempted by this?
*try tackling the
Agulhas current*

CROSS THE BAY OF BISCAY

Take on the sailing challenge that strikes fear into sailors' hearts

It is easy to look out over the open ocean and forget that the shape of the seabed hundreds of metres below can have a massive effect on surface conditions. This is certainly the case in the Bay of Biscay, the giant expanse of water that is bordered by the western coast of France and northern coast of Spain.

The bay has a fearsome reputation among sailors who have tried to cross it and limped back to harbour, battered, bruised and defeated by the mountainous seas that rise up and threaten to overcome even the sturdiest craft.

To understand the formation of these waves, consider surf on a beach. The gentle swell of the ocean is transformed into foam-filled breakers by the shelving sea floor. The same effect is found in the Bay of Biscay but on a much greater scale. The deep ocean floor of the Biscay Abyssal Plain rises up from more than 4000 metres to less than 400 metres in just a few kilometres. This severe underwater ridge stretches right across the bay and causes the mid-Atlantic swell to shorten and steepen into the marine maelstrom that unlucky sailors encounter.

High winds are required to produce the worse of these giant waves and vicious seas, and waves of over 15 metres can be created when these winds are coupled with the effect of the powerful Gulf Stream.

To avoid the worst of these waves, yachtsmen keep a westward heading as they leave the English Channel. The gradient between the deep waters of the mid-Atlantic and the shallower coastal shelf is more gradual here and so the seas are generally less severe. It is advised to cross the 10°W line of longitude before pushing the tiller over and heading south.

Storm avoidance is the key to a safe crossing, because once committed there are very few ports of refuge and long stretches of the coast become an enormous lee shore. The square-rigged ships of old couldn't sail into the wind effectively and many of them were driven ashore by gales in Biscay. Modern yachts can work to windward more efficiently and are generally advised to weather the storm rather than attempt a hazardous harbour approach.

June and July are the calmest months to cross, though with a passage time of around three days it is not unusual to experience some poor weather while crossing the bay. Complete the crossing and the wonderful cruising ground of the Spanish rias awaits, or pass around Cape Finisterre and feast on tapas in Bayona before heading south to the Med and beyond.

category
*voyages and
destinations*

location
Antarctica

difficulty
moderate–tough

time
December–February

tempted by this?
*try sailing through the
Northwest Passage*

GO EXPLORING AMONG ICEBERGS

Set sail for the frozen wastes of Antarctica

Antarctica is arguably the last great wilderness on Earth. This vast, frozen continent lies out of sight and out of mind, protected by the constant storms that roll around the Southern Ocean, the extreme temperatures and shifting ice floes that swathe its shores. The fact that it is so hard to reach and so unspoiled is its greatest attraction and, somewhat ironically, visitor numbers have rocketed from 9,000 in 1992/93 to over 46,000 in 2007/08.

The vast majority of these visitors arrive in special cruise ships but there is another, less intrusive and more environmentally friendly way to explore Antarctica.

It is possible for the most modest yacht to sail these hostile waters and return safely but the odds are stacked in favour of purpose-built expedition craft. The giant seas, numerous whales and icebergs are all hazards that could sink a yacht in seconds. Despite these risks there are many examples of 10-metre yachts cruising Antarctica for long periods.

Most vessels' explorations focus on the Antarctic Peninsula that lies beyond the tip of South America. The voyage across the Drake Passage is notoriously hazardous but once protected by the peninsula there are usually settled periods in which to discover the natural wonders of the region. The waters of Antarctica are rich with sea life and – armed with a dry suit – it is possible to swim with penguins and seals, though watch out for the leopard seals and killer whales. The fact that there are no native land animals except for the odd invertebrate is testament to the extreme hostility of the environment.

The charter yachts that sail these waters charge around US$300 a day and trips can last up to three weeks, especially if they include the crossing from South America. These craft are usually made of steel with reinforcement to protect against the impact of icebergs and the dangerous growlers that break off them and lie like mines in the sea. Inflatable boats and sea kayaks allow further up-close explorations.

The Antarctic cruising season starts in December and is over by the end of February. Temperatures at the northern edges of the Antarctic Peninsula may rise above zero but during winter coastal temperatures drop to between –10°C and –30°C. Conditions in the interior of the continent are altogether less hospitable with altitude and distance from the sea causing temperatures to drop beyond –60°C. The coldest temperature ever recorded on Earth was –89.2°C at a Russian Antarctic research station in 1983.

The extremes of weather are not limited to temperature. There are extraordinary meteorological phenomena such as diamond dust, where ice particles fall from the sky, and the setting sun can glow green or blue for hours at a time. Strong temperature contrasts near the ground can cause mirages where light is bent and ships appear to float upside down or icebergs double their size.

In May 2008, the Russian solo sailor Fedor Konyukhov completed a 26,240 km, 102-day circumnavigation of the continent as part of the promotion for the Antarctica Cup, a proposed race around the bottom of the world. Whether there will be enough adventurers who want to take on the most hostile waters in the world waits to be seen.

RACE ACROSS THE BASS STRAITS

Compete in the world famous Sydney-Hobart Race

For hundreds of sailors, Christmas Day is all about turnbuckles and sail trimming rather than turkey and all the trimmings. These are the men and women who compete in the Rolex Sydney-Hobart Race that starts on Boxing Day and involves a 1,170 km crossing from mainland Australia to the capital of the island of Tasmania.

The race was first held in 1945 and saw nine yachts set sail southwest through the Tasman Sea and across the notorious Bass Strait. The winner took six days and 14 hours to make the passage and that time has been slowly reduced in the intervening years. In 1975, an American yacht named Kialoa recorded a blistering time of two days and 14 hours that could not be beaten until 1996, and then only by 29 minutes. The current record of one day and 18 hours is held by the winner of the last four races, Wild Oats XI.

So what's the big deal about a relatively short race that takes place during the Southern Hemisphere's summer? For the answer to that, one must look beyond the Bass Strait that lies between Australia and Tasmania. Inspect an atlas and you'll see that there is nothing but open ocean to the west until the coast of South America is reached, more than half way around the world. The strait acts as a funnel for the summer storms that frequently appear at this time of year and bring giant seas as well as high winds.

The tragic events of the 1998 race secured its place in yachting history and cemented its reputation as a true challenge for the adventurous sailor. A storm of unanticipated violence swept down upon the fleet bringing with it mountainous seas and almost hurricane strength winds. Five yachts sank and six sailors, many of them highly experienced, died as rescue teams struggled to cope with the enormity of the disaster. Of the 115 boats that started, only 44 reached Hobart. As a result, the crew eligibility rules were tightened, requiring a higher minimum age and greater experience.

The events of 1998 have many haunting echoes of the 1979 Fastnet Race where 15 competitors died and 23 yachts were abandoned or sunk in a freak summer storm. Both tragedies prove that with adventure comes responsibility and risk.

The race is considered one of the world's most prestigious offshore events and attracts some of the fastest yachts on the planet that can easily complete the course in two days. The next Holy Grail is to break the 40-hour mark – and with a swing-keel and a fair wind that achievement is certainly within reach.

GET RICH SAILING A DHOW

Race a traditional boat that can really shift

category
boats

location
Dubai

difficulty
moderate

time
all year

tempted by this?
try setting sail on a Viking ship

Dhows are some of the fastest and most exciting traditional sailing boats and dhow racing as a sport is on the up. Dozens of boats compete in a series of events in Dubai with plenty of prize money on offer and thrilling high-speed races.

Dhows have carried goods and people around the waters of Arabia and beyond for more than a thousand years, but engines gradually replaced sail until, by the 1980s, there were few sailing examples left. To reverse this trend the Dubai government launched an initiative to encourage the building of new sailing dhows and in 1986 the first modern dhow race was held. More than 80 dhows compete in today's events and the sight of these ancient craft under full sail is quite unforgettable.

Each dhow is crafted by hand from teak. Power sanders may be used to take off the rough edges but the majority of the work is done with an adze and a saw. Teams of skilled Indian shipwrights can create a 20-metre dhow in a few months and prices start at around £60,000.

The carvel-built hulls of the dhow are incredibly wide in the beam but remarkably shallow, designed to trade among shoal waters and be pulled onto beaches. There is no keel or integral ballast because in the past the cargo would have been used to steady the boats. Modern dhows carry sandbags instead and these can be shifted around to keep the boats balanced. If the wind drops the sand can be tipped overboard, although if the breeze returns there is a very real risk of capsize.

Above the wide, flat hull stands the lateen rig that makes a dhow unmistakeable. The largest Dubai dhows are 20-metres long and have two masts. A spar at each masthead supports a vast expanse of canvas but tacking a dhow is a complicated procedure that can take five minutes or more. The lateen rig is more close-winded than many traditional rigs but beating into the wind is still hard work and skippers have to think carefully about how many tacks will be required to round the mark.

Dhow races are unusual for many reasons but the start procedure is almost unique with competing boats drifting at the line with no sail set. The starter's gun is the signal for sail to be hoisted and spectators watch closely to see who will get away first. The rigging is adjusted for each tack and crews of 12 or more hang precariously from the shrouds to help keep their boat as upright as possible. Speeds of well over 10 knots are common and races can be of 80 km or more.

The boats may come from humble backgrounds, but as this is Dubai the prize money is enormous with more than £1,000,000 on offer for an individual race. It all makes for intense competition and plenty of excitement on board these beautiful craft.

SAIL TO THE ISLANDS OF THE SUN

The transatlantic rally with French flair

category
races and rallies

location
transatlantic

difficulty
tricky

time
six months

tempted by this?
try joining a round-the-world rally

Yacht rallies are becoming increasingly popular with every passing year. Some sailors are happy to let experienced organizations guide and support them in their adventures, and to help them sail farther with fewer bureaucratic and safety concerns.

Of the various rallies that are run worldwide, the most unique is the Rallye Iles du Soleil or Islands of the Sun Rally. This French-run event sees a few dozen yachts congregate at the island of Madeira before sailing south to the Canaries and then heading to Senegal on the African mainland. A short hop takes the international fleet to the Cape Verde islands where participants trek through cloud forests and explore true desert islands before setting sail for Salvador on the coast of Brazil.

The fleet then sails in a series of long legs up the coast of Brazil, stopping at some of the most beautiful and remote spots. The islands of Fernando de Noronha are a particular highlight and far from the usual tourist track. This unique archipelago is hundreds of kilometres off the eastern tip of Brazil and is an ecological paradise to rival the Galapagos Islands.

Next stop is Belém at the mouth of the Amazon where the yachts ready themselves for a six-week exploration of the world's greatest river.

The six-month rally concludes as the yachts emerge back into the Atlantic, with many going on to explore the Caribbean and some continuing on through the Panama Canal and into the Pacific Ocean.

It is not just the unusual route and fascinating ports of call that makes the Islands of the Sun such a special event. The attitude of the organizers is refreshingly different too. For them, the rally is all about cultural discovery. Participants must be willing to engage with local communities and share their knowledge and experience with the people they meet. It's an incredibly relaxed, friendly affair where skippers are helped with a great deal of the complicated clearance procedures but not offered the level of 'hand-holding' seen in some other rallies.

The other unique aspect about the rally is its French-ness. Skippers' briefings or cultural tours aren't commenced until every man has had his hand shaken and every woman has been kissed on both cheeks. The briefings, when they eventually start, will deal as much with restaurant recommendations as pilotage advice and Gallic shrugs abound. It all goes to make a magical event that runs between October and March each year.

Preveza

Agnnio

onio
Pelagos
Sami

Elio-Proni

Zakynthos

Kiparissiakos
Kolpos

category
voyages and destinations

location
Greece

difficulty
moderate

time
April–October

tempted by this?
try chartering in Vietnam

ANCHOR IN THE IONIAN

Test your nerve and your patience during a Greek sailing holiday

Greece is a wonderful place to sail with blue skies, clear seas and warm winds. There are numerous islands and it's easy to escape the package holiday hotspots to enjoy some stunning bays in which to drop the hook and go for a swim. The problem is that sailors from all over the world are drawn to the beauty of this corner of the Mediterranean and things can become a little hectic during peak season.

The Ionian Sea is the epitome of all that's best and worse about sailing in Greece, and chartering here in the height of the summer is something only those with a strong sense of adventure and a good sense of humour should attempt.

The sheltered waters and normally light winds of the Ionian make it an ideal choice for a first charter and novice skippers are encouraged to join flotillas where ten or more yachts sail together, supervised by a professional skipper and hostess in a lead boat. It's a wonderful way for nervous sailors to build up their experience and confidence, and also ensures a lively social scene that's especially popular with families.

There are countless bays where yachts can swing happily around their anchor, although flotillas like to moor in a port each night. This allows the lead skipper to sleep easy in his or her bed and means that crews can step from dockside to boat after a night in the local taverna.

Mooring in the Mediterranean takes a special set of skills at which most North European yachtsmen are not very practised. Yachts need to reverse towards the harbour wall, dropping their anchor as they do so, before tying the stern to the quay. This simple system allows the maximum number of boats to be berthed together, though the execution is harder than the explanation.

Most sailors are used to going forward and find going astern a stressful experience. Things are made worse by the fact that yachts do strange things when moving backwards with the propeller acting as a paddle wheel that skews them to the side. The release of the anchor can also be problematic. Let it out too soon and you run out of chain, too late and it doesn't hold you securely. Each yacht needs to come towards the quay at right angles or their anchors become snagged on the chain of neighbouring yachts.

To make life even more difficult, these anchoring endeavours usually take place in late afternoon when the wind has sprung up. Husbands shout at wives and mothers swear at fathers while the lead skipper shouts instructions from the harbour wall. All this is conducted in front of those slightly smug crews who have already tied up.

It's a daily drama but one that rarely ends in a Greek tragedy.

CROSS THE ATLANTIC IN A BATHTUB-SIZED BOAT

Claustrophobic sailors need not apply

Big boats mean big budgets but there is another way to go adventuring on the high seas, and it is one that can earn you a place in the history books. Sailors used to cross oceans in small boats because they couldn't afford larger craft. Then, at the end of the 19th century, a trend developed for voyages in small yachts that seized the public imagination. Sail across an ocean in a small boat and there was the chance of a lucrative exhibition tour and a book deal too.

American sailors and fishermen led the way in small boat passage-making. In 1866, J.M. Hudson and F.E. Fitch crossed the Atlantic in a 7.9-metre converted lifeboat, taking 37 days to sail from New York to the English mainland. That vessel went on display at the Paris Exhibition and other sailors were inspired to take to the seas in even smaller boats.

Thomas and Joanna Crapo took 49 days to sail from Massachusetts, USA, to Penzance, UK, in 1877. Thomas had intended to make the crossing single-handed but his wife insisted on joining him. Their boat, New Bedford, was 5.9 metres and more craft of less than 6 metres soon followed their example.

William Albert Andrews crossed the Atlantic in Sapolio, a 4.4-metre boat, in 1892 and no smaller craft succeeded in replicating his voyage for a remarkable 73 years. Indeed, it was not until after the Second World War that the competition for the smallest craft to cross 'The Pond' restarted in earnest.

In 1965, the 4.1-metre Tinkerbelle, skippered by Robert Manry, sailed from Falmouth, Massachusetts to Falmouth, England. Four years later Hugo Vihlen set out from Casablanca, Morocco in April Fool, a tiny boat of just 1.8 metres. He arrived in Miami, Florida, 84 days later, having sailed 6,600 km.

British sailor Tom McNally entered the scene in 1993 when he sailed Vera Hugh across the Atlantic. Leaving Portugal in December 1992, Tom successfully navigated the 1.63-metre yacht 5,500 miles, 10,016km over the course of 134 days, arriving in Puerto Rico in May 1993. Not content with achieving this record, he added a further 1,609 km to his voyage by sailing onward to Fort Lauderdale, taking 23 days to reach mainland America.

Hugo Vihlen was not ready to surrender his title and within 12 months had crossed from Newfoundland to Ireland in a yacht just fractionally smaller. McNally has not given up and, after an abortive attempt in 1998, is still trying to find the support for a crossing in the Big C, a high-tech craft that measures just 1.16 metres.

Life aboard one of these micro cruisers is unbelievably cramped. The solo sailor sits inside a tiny enclosed cabin from which to control the steering and sails. There is no stove or toilet and only freeze-dried food can be carried. In strong winds there is no option to batten the hatch and hope for the best. These sailors may have small boats but there sense of adventure is massive.

WAKEBOARD BEHIND A TRIMARAN

Hang on tight and hope for the best

category
experience

location
worldwide

difficulty
tricky–extreme

time
minutes

tempted by this?
try kitesurfing

Wakeboarders need three things: a board, a rope and a boat to pull them. That boat is normally equipped with a large engine but a couple of adventurous French wakeboarders have shown that a 20-metre trimaran can fulfil the role of the powerboat just as well.

Brossard, the trimaran, is an incredible craft capable of extreme speeds due to the hydrofoils that lift it out of the water and above the waves. To see this giant multihull rise up from the sea is an awesome sight – but to see it towing two wakeboarders at the same time is almost unbelievable.

The men being towed were Fabienne d'Ortoli and Bruno André, both world-class kitesurfers. Kitesurfers were chosen over wakeboarders for two simple reasons: wakeboard boats provide a constant pull whereas a kite's power varies with the strength of the wind, just as the pull from Brossard would do. The riders behind Brossard would also be towed by ropes coming from the top of the mast – at a similar angle to the pull from a kite.

Wakeboarders have, however, also shown themselves adept at riding behind yachts. ABN AMROA, the Volvo 70 round-the-world racer, has towed wakeboarders including British champion Dan Nott, although it was found that slowing the boat down to a speed to allow the stunt rider to perform his most daring tricks was a problem.

Relaunching behind a tri or 21-metre racer can be problematic though these yachts often have support RIBs allowing the board riders to attempt a moving start from the support boat going at exactly the same speed as the yacht. It's a high risk manoeuvre that's only for the pros.

More modest board riders can wakeboard and waterski behind much smaller, slower craft. The fact that the tow rope comes from the top of the mast means that a great deal of upward pull is exerted, helping skiers and board riders to get up and stay up at slower speeds than would be required behind a typical tow boat. Swap the skis or wakeboard for a surfboard with its own buoyancy and you're skurfing – a combination of skiing and surfing that is possible at even slower speeds.

The mainsail halyard that hoists the sail to the top of the mast is the best rope to ski from, though it needs to be lengthened with additional lines to ensure the rider is well clear of the boat. Masts, rigging and halyards were not designed for pulling wakeboarders or anyone else and potential adrenalin junkies are advised to check that they won't be doing any damage to the boat before going wake-wandering.

REV UP IN A VOLVO 70

Race around the planet
in the world's toughest crewed race

category
races and rallies

location
worldwide

difficulty
extreme

time
nine months

tempted by this?
try racing a Transpac 52

Three sailors died in the first Whitbread Round the World Race. The event is now known as the Volvo Ocean Race but is no less dangerous or demanding and competitors still put their life on the line. That first race took place in 1973 and was inspired by pioneers such as Sir Francis Chichester and Sir Robin Knox-Johnston, who had proved that there was a public fascination with sailing around the globe.

The event has taken place every four years since that first 'Whitbread' and famous names including Sir Chay Blyth, Sir Peter Blake, Clare Francis, Paul Cayard and Grant Dalton did battle in a variety of yachts that raced within a handicapping system that allowed smaller, slower boats to compete with larger, faster craft. The 1997–98 race saw the introduction of a class rule, which meant the similar 20-metre yachts could race one another with no need to adjust results. It made life simpler for the teams and allowed the public to follow the race more easily, something that was also helped by the introduction of satellite tracking.

The Whitbread became the Volvo Ocean Race in 2001 and the 52,320-km event started from the South Coast of England and finished in Kiel, Germany. The boats took another huge leap forward in 2005 with the introduction of the Volvo Open 70 designs that incorporated the latest technology and pushed yachts and crews of 11 to the edges of endurance.

The nine-month 2008–09 Volvo, started in Alicante, Spain, in October 2008 and concluded in St Petersburg, Russia, in June 2009. The course is partially dictated by the demands of sponsors and host ports, because there is money to be made each time the yachts stop and the commercial restraints on sailing at this level cannot be ignored. The most recent course saw the teams sail over 59,545 km of the world's most treacherous seas via Cape Town, Kochi, Singapore, Qingdao, around Cape Horn to Rio de Janeiro, Boston, Galway, Goteborg and Stockholm.

Life onboard is as tough as it gets with the boats smashing through waves in a noisy, violent roller coaster ride where water cascades over the decks and any lapse of concentration can be catastrophic. Huge waves, freezing water and howling winds are all part of the job for these pro-sailors who sometimes spend more than a month at sea between ports.

Entry into one of the teams is by invitation only and a place aboard a Volvo boat marks you out as one of toughest and most skilled sailors in the world.

SURVIVE A WATERSPOUT

When wind and water go wild

category
experiences
location
worldwide
difficulty
tough
time
all year
tempted by this?
try surviving a storm

There you are, cruising the Caribbean quite happily, when all at once the laws of physics are turned upside down and water starts shooting into the sky. What you're witnessing is a waterspout and it's a natural phenomenon that has scared the life out of sailors for thousands of years.

Waterspouts are swirling vortexes of air that suck the sea into the sky and are found all over the world. Although they may look like tornadoes, most are described as non-tornadic or fair-weather waterspouts and don't have a fraction of the destructive strength of a true tornado.

For a fair-weather waterspout to form, there must be cumulus cloud over a large body of water. Warm water and relatively still, moist air provide the energy that leads to the waterspout's formation and there are tell tale signs to look out for.

Initially there is a circular area of light-coloured water around which is a darker ring. As the waterspout develops, a pattern of light and dark bands will start to spiral out from this dark area. By this point you should have dropped the sails and be motoring away as fast as possible before a swirling circle of sea spray is whipped up from the water's surface and rises up towards the cloud. The waterspout is at its most intense after joining up with the cloud base. The circling wall of spray at its base can be over 60 metres high and will kick up a large wake.

All this is bad news for sailors in the vicinity because the winds in the waterspout can reach 30 metres per second. That may not be strong enough to pluck your craft from the water as a true tornado could, but it is more than enough to knock a yacht on its side or strip the sails from the rigging. Tornadic waterspouts generally occur when a tornado moves over the water, but because nearly all tornados are found in land-locked areas of the United States these do not need to concern most sailors.

Most fair-weather waterspouts occur in the tropics where there are plentiful supplies of warm water and moist air, but they can also form in temperate areas and more than 100 are reported each year across Europe. Most take place in late summer and early autumn when sea temperatures are at their highest.

Unsurprisingly, sailors are advised to stay clear of waterspouts and warnings are given as part of weather forecasts in high-risk areas. If you are caught out, drop and secure all sails as quickly as possible and ensure that all crew are wearing safety harnesses and lifejackets. You won't be able to out-run a waterspout, but take some comfort in the knowledge that they normally last for only a few minutes before dissipating.

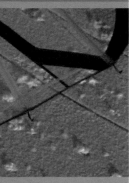

ICE IS NICE

Wings take ice sailing to new heights

category
boats

location
anywhere cold, such as the frozen lakes of North America and Europe

difficulty
tough

time
winter

tempted by this?
try kitesurfing

Adventurous sailors don't give up when the water freezes over, they just find new ways to sail even faster. Ice (or hard water as it's known within the sport) offers little resistance compared to the 'soft water' most sailors are used to, and ice yachts have been used for centuries to transport goods over frozen lakes and rivers. These original craft were sailing boats with metal runners added to their hulls and it was not long before races were held and purpose-built ice yachts were created. These craft could measure up to 15 metres and reach speeds of over 170 kilometres per hour. Top speeds of up to 240 kilometres per hour are rumoured but unconfirmed.

Ice sailing continued to evolve as a sport with lightweight, single-seater yachts becoming the vessels of choice – there has, however, been a revolution in recent years. It all started with the idea of putting a windsurf rig on a board with runners to create a relatively cheap way to go fast and have fun on the ice. The massive popularity of kitesurfing has also reached the frozen areas of Europe and North America and sailors are reaching incredible speeds equipped only with a kite, harness and pair of skates.

The greatest revolution in the sport came with the invention of the Kitewing. This cross between a kite and a sail is held in the hands but not attached to a mast or board. It stands over 2 metres tall and is normally held vertically. Sailors stand on skis, skates or snowboards and with a little practice are soon skimming across the ice at high speeds.

What sets the Kitewing apart is the fact that it can be held horizontally above the head, turning it from a sail into a wing that allows the rider to take to the air and glide for amazing distances. Skilled proponents of this remarkable new sport can perform stunts when airborne and reach remarkable heights when launching from a ramp.

The men and women who race these alternatives to traditional ice yachts compete each winter in the Ice and Snow Sailing World Championship, which has separate classes for sleds powered by windsurf sails, kites and handheld Kitewings.

The makers of the Kitewing also produce the Wave Warrior, a similar handheld wing that is designed for use on 'soft water' with a kitesurf board. Its 7.5-metre square foil can be flown in anything from 16 to 36 knots of wind and jumps of 3 metres are reported from 30-centimetre waves.

Such a blurring of the lines between land and sea, sailing and flying has the yachting purists in a state. Surely this cannot be sailing, they say; but what else do you call a sport where wind and water (whether hard or soft) are the only requirements?

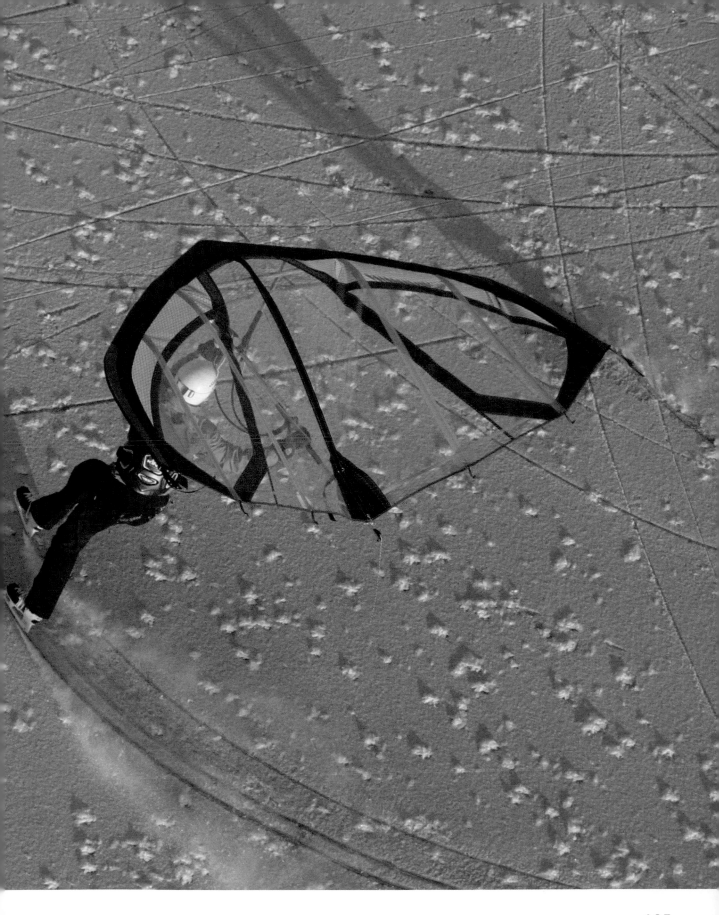

Peru

●Lake Titicaca

Bolivia

REACH THE HEIGHTS IN SOUTH AMERICA

Lake Titicaca is still waiting to be explored

Lake Titicaca is the largest freshwater lake in South America and sitting at 3,812 metres above sea level is one of the highest navigable lakes in the world. The lake is remarkable in all aspects, covering an area of 8,288 square kilometres and reaching depths of up to 305 metres.

As a sailing destination, Lake Titicaca is reserved for only the most adventurous. A few pleasure craft are kept on its shores but there is no established yacht charter industry, and so if you want to sail a modern yacht you'll have to bring your own.

That's exactly what the great adventurer Tristan Jones did in 1975 when he sailed Sea Dart, his 6.4-metre bilge keeled cutter, on these waters on top of the world. Jones's incredible voyage had started on the Dead Sea, the lowest navigable waters on earth and he sailed his tiny vessel across the oceans before reaching Callao on the Peruvian coast. From there he had to truck the boat over perilous mountain passes to reach the mighty Lake Titicaca and so set a record for sailing on the lowest and highest lakes in the world. Jones spent months cruising the six main islands and countless other islets, bays and beaches.

If you don't have the time, money or patience to sail and truck your own yacht to the lake, you may have to do what the indigenous people have done for thousands of years and make a vessel out of the totora reeds that grow on the banks. These reeds have literally supported the local population since around 2000BC. Their roots are edible while the reeds themselves are used to build houses and boats. They are also matted into vast floating islands that small communities live on throughout the year.

The reed boats are remarkable feats of nautical engineering, using the natural absorbency of the plant to create integral ballast. These boats are still used for fishing and local transport and a recent archaeological project saw the construction of a 14.3-metre reed boat that was capable of supporting the weight of more than 10 family cars.

Remember to watch out for the Bolivian Navy when sailing the waters of Lake Titicaca on your reed yacht. Bolivia has no coastline but the lake forms part of the border with neighbouring Peru and naval craft carry out exercises on its waters.

When you've finished your explorations of this deep blue lake with its mountainous backdrop you may decide to follow the example of Tristan Jones and ship your boat to the head of the Corumba River in Brazil and continue your journey eastwards to the Atlantic down the Paraguay and Paraná rivers to Buenos Aires.

CROSS AN OCEAN IN A BEACH CAT

Dare you try this low budget, high risk adventure?

category
voyages and destinations

location
Atlantic/Pacific

difficulty
extreme

time
16 days +

tempted by this?
try windsurfing across the Pacific

The first adventurers to cross the world's oceans did so on small vessels that were exposed to the elements. The design of boats has changed a great deal over the centuries but the challenge of sailing the world's seas in an open boat has not diminished. It is a challenge that only the most daring adventurers accept, and the bravest of them all must surely be Alessandro Di Benedetto, who has crossed both the Atlantic and the Pacific on the sort of catamaran that you're most likely to see pulled up on the beach of a holiday resort.

These beach catamarans have no accommodation at all and offer no protection from the elements. They are little more than a pair of canoes held apart by crossbeams across which a mesh trampoline is stretched. They are very fast and very, very wet. Exactly the sort of boat you do *not* want to be aboard for weeks at a time.

Cooking is impossible, remaining dry is a fantasy and all equipment must be carried in watertight containers lashed to the deck. Toilet arrangements are non-existent and saltwater sores are inevitable.

Alessandro first crossed the Atlantic in an open catamaran in 1992. It was a two-handed passage and he sailed with his father, taking 16 days to reach Martinique from the Canary Islands. Ten years later he made the same passage in 28 days, but this time he was solo. It was an incredible achievement that reflected a level of bravery and seamanship that most sailors can only dream about. Alessandro had to drop the sails while he slept because no self-steering system could be trusted to keep a steady course and avoid a capsize or pitchpole, which would have spelled disaster or even death. He made it in one piece and in 2006 went on to sail singlehanded in a purpose built, 5.5-metre open catamaran across the Pacific. The epic voyage from Japan to San Francisco took 62 days.

The hazards of such passages were shown all too clearly by Alessandro's brother, Francesco, who attempted a solo beach cat Atlantic crossing in 2007. He was hit by a storm when seven days out of Gran Canaria, his open 6-metre Tornado catamaran capsized and all his possessions were washed away. 'I had nothing,' he later reported. 'Imagine [just] myself, the boat, the mast and two sails.'

Francesco lost his glasses and contact lenses and could hardly see to the end of his boat. He had a compass but no torch, and so could only guess at his course during the night. Despite having an emergency radio beacon, he decided to push on, surviving for 12 days without food or water in the hope of coming across another vessel. It was a brave effort but in the end he had to send out a Mayday and was a rescued by a merchant ship.

Southampton

The Solent • **Cowes**

Isle of Wight

category
races and rallies

location
the Solent, UK

difficulty
moderate

time
August

tempted by this?
try competing for the King's Cup

COMPETE IN COWES

Take part in Britain's biggest regatta

Take a small stretch of water with an island to the south and the British mainland to the north and fill it with 1,000 yachts and 8,500 crew. Add strong tides, unpredictable weather and a generous splash of socializing. The result is Cowes Week, the biggest and best sailing event of the year for the UK yachting community.

More than 1,000 bottles of Pimms are drunk by the sailors and 80,000 spectators that come to watch this sailing spectacular. Some 10,000 bacon sandwiches are then consumed the morning after to fortify skippers and crew for another day of battle on the water.

Cowes Week was first held in 1826 when yachting suddenly became fashionable due to the enthusiasm of King George IV. Two races were held under the auspices of the Royal Yacht Club, now known as the Royal Yacht Squadron (or simply 'The Squadron' to the upper echelons who form its ranks).

The first Cowes Week lasted for just two days but the event grew over the years and the number of classes gradually expanded as smaller yachts were built and sailing became more accessible to those without limitless funds. The classes continue to proliferate and there can now be up to 40 different starts a day. The variety of yachts sharing the same water is part of Cowes Week's charm. Traditional Sunbeams and Seaview Mermaids race alongside hi-tech Laser SB3s and 1720 keelboats. Carbon and Kevlar racers sail across the Solent with yachts that for the other 51 weeks of the year are used for family cruising.

Some of the biggest, fastest yachts from all over the world come to Cowes Week because the event is famous throughout the world and Open 60 yachts race fully crewed, often with a smattering of celebrities on board to attract coverage for the sponsors. There are one-design classes for open day boats and popular designs such as the Contessa 32 whereas mixed fleets group yachts by speed and size to ensure close racing.

The sheer number of yachts on the water makes competing in Cowes Week something of an adventure: as well as the 1,000 competitors, there are hundreds of boats that come to watch and have a habit of getting in the way. Throw in the fact that the Solent is one of the busiest areas in the world for commercial shipping and you have a recipe for excitement and adrenalin. Underwater hazards include rock ledges, wrecks and sandbanks, and the tides are notoriously tricky.

It all makes for a wonderful week of hard partying and even harder sailing. Taking part is easy because many sailing schools and charter companies enter yachts each year.

Macapá

Alter Do Chão

category
*voyages and
destinations*

location
Brazil

difficulty
tricky

time
all year

tempted by this?
*try joining an
Amazonian rally*

SAIL UP THE AMAZON

Discover a tropical paradise in the heart of the jungle

The Amazon truly deserves its status as the greatest river in the world. More water flows between its banks than through the next top ten rivers put together – and it is this fact that makes sailing up the Amazon such a challenge.

The river's drainage basin spreads for more than 6,475,000 square kilometres, and combined with heavy equatorial downpours creates a strong current that can be very difficult to counter. The harsh reality is that to sail up the Amazon is incredibly hard work, unless you have an exceptionally fast yacht that can make way against the currents that can run at more than 4 knots. The sensible sailors motor up the Amazon and sail down it.

The current brings with it other dangers – quite literally. Islands of vegetation can be torn away by the water and sent spiralling out to sea. These masses of leaves, branches and soil can be larger than a tennis court and represent a difficulty that most sailors will have not encountered before: navigation is much more challenging when the land is moving too!

As well as floating islands, there are drifting logs and tree trunks that stop a yacht dead in the water. A metal guard around the propeller can offer some protection and is highly recommended for a dinghy's outboard engine. Other essential kit includes a machete for hacking off the vegetation that quickly becomes wrapped around anchor chains. Towns and cities are few and far between up the Amazon and so it is vital to carry enough fuel, water and spares. Break down and the nearest mechanic is probably a plane ride away.

The rewards for those who overcome all these difficulties are immense, especially if you escape the widest (and frankly quite dull) stretches of river. Venture into the tributaries and explore among the backwaters to discover a land and a people that have been little changed by time and where a gentle, if timid, welcome is almost assured. There are rare reports of thefts and Sir Peter Blake was killed while exploring the river, and so caution is advised here as in almost any other corner of the world.

The wildlife of the Amazon is breathtaking with parrots taking the place of seagulls. The river may be full of piranha but these little fish have had a bad press and are very rarely dangerous. After four weeks heading up river, you reach Alter Do Chão, the Caribbean of the Amazon, an area of stunning, beach fringed islands and that few visitors ever see.

The river is 6,400 km long with countless smaller rivers feeding into it. Sailing it all would take a lifetime, but remember not to rush the journey upstream. With 4 knots of current behind you, it doesn't take long to get out to sea again.

Dorset

Weymouth

Portland Bill

category
experiences

location
Dorset, UK

difficulty
tricky

time
all year

tempted by this?
*try venturing around
Ardnamurchan*

RACE AROUND PORTLAND BILL

Take on the tide on the south coast of England

It is true that time and tide wait for no man, but it is also true that the tide must go around the many headlands that obstruct its path. This is certainly the case along the south coast of England where the rocky edifice of Portland Bill protrudes into the English Channel at the southern tip of a 6-km island connected to the mainland by Chesil Beach.

A bill is a local name for a promontory and the obstruction caused by the Portland stone of Portland Bill causes the tide to rush around it at speeds of up to 7 knots. The eddies that form around the Bill collide in an area of relatively shallow water and the waves that are created have no rhyme or reason in their shape or direction. These are boiling seas where the water comes from three places at once to create massive pyramids that rise up and threaten to overcome even the strongest vessel. Countless ships have been lost in this marine maelstrom, which lies in wait for sailors heading to and from the stunning scenery and busy fishing ports of the West Country.

To make matters worse, the delightfully named Shambles Bank – another area of shallow water – channels the tide towards Portland Bill. This combination of factors creates the notorious Portland Race and tidal flows within this band of seething sea can reach a staggering 10 knots.

These dangerous conditions are exacerbated yet further by the swells that quickly built up in the Channel. Add the effects of strong winds blowing against the flow of the tide and you have a recipe for pure chaos where the sea seems alive and walls of white water explode from nowhere.

This is no place to venture in a yacht and sensible skippers give Portland Bill a wide berth of at least 8 km, and double that in rough weather. People tempted to cut the corner and shave some time off their passage should beware the currents that surround the Race and can draw all but the most powerful craft inexorably into its deadly waters.

An alternative to this long detour does exist but only adventurous skippers blessed with settled weather should attempt it. Those with a steely nerve and a fair forecast can slip between the ravages of the Portland Race and the shore of the Bill itself in calm waters, thus cutting miles off their coastal journey. This adventurous piece of pilotage requires precise timing and a keen eye on the chart. Arrive at the tip of the Bill too early or too late and instead of an easy passage keeping 200m from the shore you will find yourself being sucked into the race and possibly joining the dozens of mariners who have failed to win 'the race' and so lost their lives.

BECOME A SUPERYACHT SKIPPER

Sail a beautiful boat
in stunning waters and get rich too

category
experiences

location
worldwide

difficulty
tricky

time
all year

tempted by this?
*try chartering the
Maltese Falcon*

There are many ways to make a living out of sailing but becoming the captain of a superyacht must be one of the most glamorous and can be remarkably adventurous too.

The superyacht market has enjoyed a massive boom in recent years and seems impervious to the worst financial upheavals. Multimillionaires are having to wait in line to collect the yacht of their dreams, and although most boats have massive engines rather than masts, there are a significant number of luxurious sailing craft built each year, and each of them needs a skipper.

The captain of a superyacht has an apparently simple job: sail where he or she's told to sail and ensure the owner and guests are happy. The reality can be a good deal more complicated, especially with millionaires who don't understand boats and are used to getting their own way. The average oligarch may be slow to appreciate that tides or weather forecasts may require plans to be modified and will look dimly on having to rearrange their plans because you need to replace a part or stitch a sail. They expect their pride and joy to be gleaming from the outside and immaculate on the inside, and so don't get into the superyacht business unless you like cleaning.

To reach the position of captain you'll need to work your way up the ranks, gathering experience and qualifications as you go. To become qualified as the master of a vessel less than 200 gross tonnes that can sail an unlimited area, you first need to obtain Yachtmaster Ocean theory and practical tests as well earning a Maritime and Coastguard Agency certificate of competency. Next comes basic training on 'big boats' and a radio operator's certificate. With all this completed you still have to pass a tricky oral exam before earning your 'ticket'. This is just the start of the superyacht career ladder with the best of the best going on to become masters of yachts up to 3,000 gross tonnes.

With the experience and qualifications under your belt, it's time to look for a job. Some owners only spend a few weeks of the year on board, leaving you with your own private yacht for the rest of the time. Others virtually live onboard and expect round the clock attention.

Try and find out about their sailing plans. Although a majority of owners just want a floating hotel, some have a more adventurous spirit and want to explore the far-flung islands of the Pacific or watch the wildlife of the Tierra del Fuego. Choose wisely and you'll be exploring the world in luxury while earning a good salary with free food and lodging and no tax to pay.

EAT OYSTERS
IN FRENCHMAN'S CREEK

Let your taste buds
take you on a cruise of Cornwall

Cornwall

Helford

category
experiences

location
Cornwall, UK

difficulty
simple

time
all year

tempted by this?
*try eating flying fish
at sea*

Cracking open oysters in an inlet best known as the title of a book is a culinary and literary adventure, rather than an act of nautical derring-do. To combine the pleasures of the palate and the mind, you'll need a boat, a copy of *Frenchman's Creek* by Daphne du Maurier and a blunt knife. A bottle of Muscadet and a loaf of good bread are advised but not essential.

Frenchman's Creek is a small and assuming offshoot of the Helford River that lies at the north-eastern edge of the Lizard peninsula in Cornwall. The cruise along the West Country coast takes you to such places as Dartmouth, Salcombe, Plymouth, Fowey and Falmouth – all of which have delightful rivers lying beyond them. The farthest west and least spoilt of these rivers is the Helford, whose small beaches and wood-lined banks seem to have resisted the passing of time, changing little over the years.

If you don't have time to sail so far west, charter a yacht in Falmouth or hire a dayboat on the Helford. Equipped with the essentials for your epicurean adventure you must first check the tide table and then plot a course for Porth Navas, a nearby creek and the home of the Duchy of Cornwall Oyster Farm. At high water you may be able to go alongside the old stone quay, otherwise you'll need to anchor off and go ashore by dinghy. If there is less than 1.6 metres of tide you'll find yourself stuck in the mud.

Oysters have been farmed on the Helford River for generations and are regarded as some of the best in the world. Native oysters are available from September to April whereas Pacifics can be had all year round, except during exceptionally hot summers.

The oyster farm is happy to sell to the public, and with plans for a new shop should be able to provide you with a special oyster knife and maybe even a chain-mail glove to protect your hand.

Buy a dozen of the finest oysters you can afford, slip back out to the main river and swing round to the west with your back to the sea. On your port bow you'll see a small inlet and this is the creek made famous in the historical novel written by du Maurier in 1942. Set in Cornwall during the reign of Charles II, it tells the story of a love affair between an impulsive English lady and a French pirate. It's a swashbuckling yet romantic tale and where better to read it than in the creek where the pirate hid his vessel.

First, however, you'll need to suspend the wine over the stern to chill while you 'shuck' the oysters and cut the bread. Now relax as you slurp the freshest imaginable shellfish and feast on du Maurier's lavish prose.

SURVIVE A STORM

Could a parachute or fish oil
help save you in a gale?

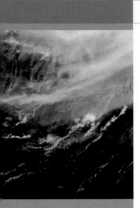

Adventurous sailors are almost certain to find themselves caught out in extreme weather and there comes a time when sailing becomes survival. The true power of the wind and the waves at their most ferocious is impossible to imagine. Seas are transformed into landscapes of mountainous water where breaking seas power down the front of towering waves. When the wind reaches monstrous speeds, the surface of the sea simply can't resist its force and becomes airborne, flying horizontally and blurring the boundary between water and air.

A variety of survival techniques can be adopted when caught out in such severe weather and choosing the best one depends on where you are, your boat, crew and how long the tempest is expected to last.

As the wind grows stronger, the sails a yacht is flying become smaller and smaller. Eventually the smallest conventional sails will be replaced by tiny storm jibs and tri sails, strips of canvas designed to allow the yacht to keep moving, and so be able to be steered, while providing a minimal surface area.

If there is enough sea room it often makes sense to run before the wind, though going in the same direction as the wind and waves carries its own dangers. If a yacht accelerates too quickly down the face of a wave it can pitchpole, flipping over with all the obvious dangers to the vessel and crew. The only way to slow the boat down is to tow objects through the water: long mooring warps may do the trick and anchor chain can help.

Things may get so bad that even the storm sails may make the yacht over-canvassed and the unlucky skipper has to take down all sail and run under bare poles. The force of the wind on the hull and rigging of a yacht is enough to drive it along surprisingly quickly and sea anchors are used to try and limit the drift and control the angle at which the yacht lies to the waves.

Those who have survived storms at sea recommend deploying an underwater parachute that's attached with a bridle to the front and middle of the boat, thus keeping it at a slight angle to the oncoming waves. Then there is nothing to do but batten down the hatches and wait.

Before retiring below, it is wise to remove anything that can be stripped from the deck because the waves have enough power to bend metal and carry away anything that's not permanently fixed.

Fishermen of old used to tow a leaking barrel of fish oil in the hope that the oil would help prevent waves from breaking over their boat. An environmentally unfriendly alternative for modern mariners involves puncturing an oilcan, although the effectiveness of pouring oil on troubled waters has yet to be proved.

BE THE 18TH MAN

Get close to the action on an America's Cup yacht

category
races and rallies

location
worldwide

difficulty
extreme

time
every 2–5 years

tempted by this?
*try watching
phosphorescent
dolphins*

Imagine sitting behind Lewis Hamilton as he races in a Grand Prix: you're in the heart of the action but don't have to do any of the work. That's exactly the experience enjoyed by the 18th man on board an America's Cup yacht.

These most perfectly positioned spectators sit at the back of the boat and live every second of the race along with the crews. They are tucked out of the way behind the pit where winches are ground and tacticians bark orders over the sound of creaking carbon fibre. It's no easy ride as the yachts heel and pound through the waves with water breaking over the non-sailing crew, whose only job is to soak in every sight and sound of this once-in-a-lifetime experience.

The creation of the 18th man was a work of marketing genius. Few will ever be able to enjoy it but those lucky enough to sail on one of these high-tech racers cannot fail to be impressed. Owners, sponsors, politicians and power brokers are all given a ticket to ride, along with members of the media who never fail to sing the praises of the team that allowed them this unforgettable opportunity.

These VIPs are in a unique position to witness the way a crew of 17 can transform a 24-tonne piece of carbon fibre into a flying machine. These are the best professional sailors in the world, bar none, and each of them knows that the smallest mistake will cost them dearly.

Each has a specific role to play with the athletic foredeck crew handling the vast sails and dangling from the end of the giant spinnaker pole. The grinders provide the muscle, each bent over pedestal winches, known as coffee grinders, which can be linked together via complicated gears to hoist the sails or sheet in the sails. The trimmers are in charge of the sheets and know exactly how each sail should be set for maximum speed. The afterguard consists of the helmsman, skipper, tactician, strategist and navigator although one person can fulfil several roles. These are the brains of the boat and the 18th man is perfectly positioned to witness how they read the waves and wind while engaging in mind games with their competitors, which are played out at breakneck speed.

The role of 18th man is not without its dangers. America's Cup yachts are at the cutting edge of technology and breakages are common. Masts snap and come crashing down to the deck and two yachts have sunk in recent events.

The risks are worth it of course, because the lucky passenger experiences a sailing adventure that the rest of us can only dream of.

China

Vietnam

Ha Long
Bay

category
*voyages and
destinations*

location
Vietnam

difficulty
simple

time
all year

tempted by this?
*try cruising the Cape
Verdes*

EXPLORE THE TOWERS
OF HA LONG BAY

Discover a unique cruising ground

In a quiet corner of South East Asia lies one of the most spectacular cruising grounds in the world. Ha Long Bay is in the Gulf of Tonkin, where the north-eastern coast of Vietnam meets the most south-westerly coast of China. Its coastline stretches for some 120 km and covers an area of more than 1,553 square kilometres.

What makes Ha Long Bay such a unique place to sail are the 2,000 islets that rise up from its warm waters. Each of these limestone monoliths is topped with a lush miniature jungle and it is this combination of sheer rock faces and lush vegetation that makes the area so remarkable.

The war kept visitors away from this exciting country for decades but Vietnam now has a strong and growing tourist industry. Many of these visitors come to Ha Long Bay for a day trip or short cruise. There is a well-established route and the more popular areas can become crowded at any time of the year.

Sailors have the great luxury of being able to set their own course, and with so many islands to visit they can soon leave the crowds of tripper boats in their wake. A well provisioned boat is essential if sailing in the region because facilities are few and far between once the tourist hotspots are left behind. One thing that is not in short supply is fish, and you are never far from a fishing village where you can buy the freshest fish that are caught (and farmed) in these waters.

Yacht charter operators are just waking up to the opportunities of Vietnam and other relatively undiscovered corners of Asia, and chartering here does have a truly adventurous feel to it. It pays to research the weather, however, because Ha Long Bay experiences a cold, dry winter with frequent mists and a hot, moist summer. More than 2 metres of rain falls each year, though these tropical downpours rarely last long.

When cruising among the islands, an inflatable dinghy is vital for close up explorations. The limestone outcrops are full of caves, some of which can only be entered at low tide and many containing secret lakes. The increase in visitor numbers, however, is causing problems for the delicate ecology of the region. Cave openings are being expanded to allow easy access for the boat loads of visitors and the engines of these same boats are polluting the water. Hopefully considerate yachtsmen and women will have a less harmful impact on this stunning area and the mysterious towers that rise from the sea.

GET ALL FIRED UP ON A GUNBOAT

Luxury and speed combine on this high-tech catamaran

category
boats

location
worldwide

difficulty
moderate

time
all year

tempted by this?
try racing a maxi catamaran

The ultimate sailing adventure requires the ultimate yacht: one that is fast, fun and capable of going anywhere. All sailors have their own idea of a perfect vessel but few will tick as many boxes as a Gunboat.

These remarkable catamarans combine a multitude of appealing features. What sets them apart from the competition is their speed and this is a result of high-tech construction and some very clever design. Gunboats are extremely light with all excess weight engineered out of each component. Nomex, carbon and Kevlar are used throughout with structures made of honeycomb cores that are both incredibly strong and a fraction of the weight of their wooden or fibreglass equivalents. Even the furniture is cored with honeycomb to save vital ounces.

These modern materials are coupled with a powerful rig that allows Gunboats to cover 450 or even 650 km in a day. This speed is maintained while the yacht stays on an even keel, allowing crew to live horizontally while their monohull mates are at a constant angle.

Daggerboards extend from each hull to give the Gunboat additional stability, though they can be lifted to allow access to the shallowest of waters.

One big problem experienced by many catamaran owners is the inability to see what's going on from the large aft deck. Gunboats counter this with a dedicated forward cockpit at the base of the mast. The skipper can helm from here and all sail controls are in easy reach; there is also much improved visibility.

With the working cockpit out of the way, the rest of the boat is for pure pleasure. Catamarans make ideal living platforms where the indoors and outdoors can be integrated. The saloon and deck are all the same level and there's always a 360-degree view.

The capability of catamarans to cope with severe storms is an issue that is often raised, but Gunboat's designers say that her safety lies in her speed, which carries her quickly out of harm's way. Being caught out in heavy weather is inevitable during any ocean adventure and the Gunboat team claim that with her daggerboards up, the round-bottomed hulls will skate sideways along waves preventing a capsize while the long, high bows offer plenty of buoyancy.

A Kevlar reinforced underbody makes for a tough hull and six water-tight bulkheads limit the ingress of any water. The foam core of the hull also acts as reserve buoyancy, allowing the builders to boast that 'even with the unthinkable, it remains unsinkable'.

A range of Gunboats have been built (14.6–27.4 metres in length). Such high performance doesn't come cheap but several of these stunning cats are available to charter.

HITCHHIKE AROUND THE WORLD BY BOAT

If you're willing and able you can circumnavigate for free

category
voyages and destinations

location
worldwide

difficulty
moderate

time
all year

tempted by this?
try joining a round-the-world rally

There was a time when the yachts that sailed around the world were almost all less than 12 metres and sailed by husband and wife crews. Those slim, seaworthy craft were easily managed by two people and could feel crowded with additional crew.

Times change, however, and today's average world cruising boat is wider and longer and so harder to sail. The 'mister and missus' crew has stayed the same but instead of being young ocean gypsies they may well be retirees who would welcome a helping hand on long ocean passages. If you can offer a small amount of sailing skill and a great deal of time you can hitchhike your way around the oceans of the world.

Qualifications help and a 'ticket' showing that you've passed one of the Royal Yachting Association courses (or an international equivalent) may help you secure a berth. More important is a friendly face and the ability to get along with strangers in the confined environment of a yacht. It is a lot to ask and you can all too easily allow the glamour of sailing to distract you from the fact that you can be imprisoned in something the size of a caravan for weeks at a time with very little privacy and no means of escape. The caravan is often at an angle and constantly moving – and fresh water is always a limited commodity. The view is great and there's plenty of exercise and fresh air, but not everyone can cope with conditions ten times more claustrophobic than those experienced by Big Brother contestants.

If you can cope with all of that and the idiosyncrasies of your fellow humans while willingly standing watch at night, sharing the cooking and cleaning and all the other onboard jobs, you should be welcomed with open arms.

Finding a boat with a space onboard involves self-promotion and shoe leather. to start, you need to get to one of the ocean crossroads where yachts gather before long passages. The list is long and includes ports such as Las Palmas in Gran Canaria, Gibraltar, English Harbour in Antigua, either end of the Panama Canal, Darwin, Singapore and Galle in Sri Lanka.

You need an email address or better still a website detailing your skills and experience and why you'd make the perfect shipmate. Put up posters offering your services around the marinas and bars and then start walking the pontoons and asking at each and every boat. If you do find a berth, spend as much time onboard as possible before you set sail, because it's better to discover an owner's foibles while still tied to the dock than 150 km out to sea with a two-week passage ahead.

COMPETE IN THE MINI-TRANSAT

Fly across the Atlantic aboard a pocket rocket

Many sailors dream of competing in a major offshore race onboard an Open 60 yacht but few can raise the millions of pounds of sponsorship required to make those dreams come true. Fortunately there is class of yacht designed for those with less cash but plenty of nerve. Welcome to the world of the Mini 6.50 where the boats are small (6.5-metre) but incredibly powerful. It is an 'open' class where there are limits to the dimensions and weights of the vessel, but almost anything else goes.

This openness allows sailors to adopt an approach to fit their budget. If the sponsors are standing by with their chequebooks, expect carbon fibre, canting keels and wing masts. A home-built plywood hull, however, may be more sensible for skippers who need to sell their car and cash-in their savings to fund a campaign. There are numerous second-hand boats about and there is a way into the sport for everyone.

And what a sport it is, in which small boats take on big oceans at high speeds. The highlight is the biennial Mini-Transat race that goes from Charente Maritime in Western France, via the Portuguese island of Madeira, to Salvador de Bahia in Brazil. This race is 7,800 km of single-handed ocean sailing that tests competitors' skills and endurance to the limit. The course passes through the northeast trade winds, the dreaded Doldrums and the southeast trades, and ensures that every sort of condition will be experienced. Taking part in this event is at the heart of all the skippers' campaign and the boats are often referred to as Mini-Transats.

Mini 6.50 yachts are scaled down versions of Open 60s with wide sterns that improve stability and allow them to skim across the waves. They have huge downwind sails called gennakers, which allow them to maintain speeds in excess of 10 knots. Designers are always trying something new to make the boats go faster and many of these successful innovations later appear on larger boats. As well as these prototype vessels, there's a production division that allows identical boats to be bought off the shelf, again reducing costs.

In the years between transatlantic races, there are a series of events that see these pocket rockets being raced both solo and two-handed around the coast of Europe. Survive the circuit and you may be ready to follow in the wake of Ellen MacArthur and almost all the French ocean racing stars who learned their trade aboard a Mini.

Cornwall

Isles of Scilly

SAIL TO THE SCILLIES

Venture west to discover a subtropical island paradise

category
voyages and destinations

location
UK

difficulty
moderate

time
spring and summer

tempted by this?
try exploring the Galapagos Islands

The Isles of Scilly lie in the open Atlantic, more than 30 km from the southwest tip of mainland Britain. One may expect such far-flung islands to be little more than weather-beaten rocks, ravaged by the might of the sea that surrounds them – instead they are a haven of flora and fauna that benefit from the warming effect of the Gulf Stream, which banishes frosts and creates a subtropical paradise.

The 48 islands that make up the archipelago cover an area of more than 103 square kilometres. Six of them are inhabited and a further 18 support vegetation. Together they make up a cruising wonderland where crystal clear waters are teeming with marine life and a multitude of bays and beaches await the adventurous sailor.

Reaching the Isles of Scilly is the first challenge to be overcome. The exposed waters of the Western Approaches quickly become whipped up in strong winds, and so a settled forecast is essential when setting off from mainland England. The importance of getting the forecast right is doubly important, because the islands offer no all-weather anchorage that is protected from every direction. Get caught out in rough weather and changing winds and you may be forced to find a new anchorage in the height of the gale. To make matters worse, the fine sand and weed-covered rocks offer unreliable holding.

Once among the islands there is no time to relax because the numerous rocks and shallows demand careful pilotage, and the currents run strongly through the channels. Pick your way carefully, using the charts and numerous transit lines, and you'll be able to reach beautiful bays where palm trees really do sway in the breeze.

St Mary's is the largest island and the centre of community life on Scilly. Tresco is wonderland for gardeners and Tean is a haven for ornithologists, though it is off limits from April to July when ringed plovers and terns are nesting. Venture ashore and you'll be reminded of the rules during an aerial bombardment of angry birds.

St Agnes and Gugh, along with the other islands, make the most of their unusually mild climate to grow flowers, and you can be sure that the first daffodils of the season will have come from Scilly.

Pick your way around hazards such as Rascal's Ledge, Crow Bar and Lubber's Rock to find your own corner of this spectacular group of islands. Wander the unspoiled beaches and dine on the freshest seafood, but always keep a weather-eye out for a change in conditions and be ready for a quick run back to the safety of the mainland.

GET BIG AIR!

Launch yourself into the sky with a sail

category
boats

location
worldwide

difficulty
extreme

time
all year

tempted by this?
try flying with a Kite Wing

Professional windsurfing competitions are divided into three distinct groups: slalom, freestyle and wave. Of these, wave events are by far the most exciting and dramatic. In fact, these 'big air' challenges have literally taken sailing to new heights. The requirements for a successful wave event are simple: lots of wind, huge waves and a group of tanned, fearless gods of the windsurfing world.

When it comes to big breakers, it is those with a sail on their board who lead the way. Indeed, it was windsurfers who first rode the largest surf on the planet. Waves such as the notorious Jaws on the Hawaiian island of Maui simply cannot be tackled from a standing start. This meant that traditional surfers could only look on in envy (or relief) as their windsurfing cousins raced down walls of thundering water over 15 metres high. It was only with the introduction of jet-skis that surfers without sails could tackle these monsters, by being towed onto their towering faces.

Windsurf wave riding consists of getting out through the surf, and then turning around and riding the waves back towards the shore. It is on the outward journey that these men and women with small boards and big sails take to the sky. The waves act as launch pads, propelling the windsurfers skywards. Once airborne there are a variety of tricks that can be performed. Forward and backward rotating loops (somersaults to the layperson) are the wave riders' stock in trade. Arms and legs can be flung around mid-air to add to the excitement. A double forward loop is something to write home about and a triple loop is what every wave windsurfer wants for Christmas – a few have attempted it but no one has yet succeeded.

If you fancy getting some big air yourself, be aware that the road is long, hard and very wet! Windsurf boards don't have a rudder, unlike almost all other sailing craft, and the technique of leaning the sail forward and backwards to steer can be hard to master. Once able to direct the board, novices have to leave the security of a board that will bear their weight in favour of one that sinks as soon as it stops moving – another strange concept for most sailors. Next comes practice and nerves of steel. Oh, and you'll need some big surf and an offshore wind, too.

SAIL AROUND THE WORLD

Circumnavigating Planet Earth is the greatest adventure of all

category
voyages and destinations

location
worldwide

difficulty
tough

time
50 days +

tempted by this?
try sailing around Antarctica

There are two ways to sail around the world: as a continuous, non-stop passage or with breaks between legs. The first is the reserve of racing yachtsmen and women and those who wish to set records. The second seems the more sensible option for cruising sailors. After all, why sail all the way to Australia and not stop for a while to say 'G'day'.

The first person to circle the globe by boat is generally accepted to be Ferdinand Magellan in 1519–22. The expedition he led certainly completed the global circuit, although Magellan actually died a year before its conclusion. It was Francis Drake who led the first successful circumnavigation under one leader, returning to Britain in 1580 after three years at sea. Between 1768 and 1779, James Cook made two circumnavigations and almost completed a third.

It was not until the end of the 19th century that a single-handed voyage around the world was attempted. Joshua Slocum set off from the United States of America in 1895 on board Spray, an 11.2-metre sloop that many considered unsuitable for the task. Slocum's voyage of 73,600 km took him to Europe, South America, Australia, Indonesia and Africa before sailing into Newport, Rhode Island, on 27 June, 1898. The adventures he had along the way are described in *Sailing Alone Around The World,* one of the great pieces of sailing literature and one that still inspires sailors more than a century later.

The possibility of sailing non-stop around the world was raised after the epic voyage of Sir Francis Chichester onboard Gipsy Moth IV. Chichester stopped once in Australia to modify his boat but his voyage (1966–67) caught the public imagination and the next year a competition was held to see who could be the first person to circle the world, without stopping or any outside assistance.

The Golden Globe Race attracted a strange mix of sailors and yachts and it was Robin Knox-Johnston, playing the part of the tortoise rather than the hare, who came home first after more than 300 days at sea aboard the 8.4-metre Suhali.

If you're happy to stop, the Suez and Panama canals offer useful short cuts and allow a circumnavigation that avoids the great capes of Horn and Good Hope. Thousands of cruising yachts are circumnavigating the planet at any one time and some skippers take many years before they cross the route of their outward passage and 'tie the knot'.

GET SEXY
WITH A WALLY

Sail the true Esense of style

There are a few yachts that can cause your heart to race just by looking at them. Esense, a one-off Wally 143, is one such craft and is arguably the sexiest yacht in the world.

Built for an incredibly rich private owner, Esense is the epitome of style and what's more, she sails like a dream. The teak of her expansive decks is gently contoured so that no hard edges break her stunning lines. All the sailing machinery – the cleats, winches and runners – are hidden beneath the deck and controlled electronically. The systems are so sophisticated that she can be operated almost single-handed despite being 43 metres long. Stern- and bow-thrusters assist docking and a massive 550hp Caterpillar engine provides the drive to take her to 14 knots.

But a yacht like this was built to be sailed. At the touch of a button on the central control panel, the mainsail rises up the towering 57-metre carbon mast. The work of another fingertip unfurls the self-tacking blade jib. In a moment Esense is accelerating as she leans away from the wind, balanced by a six-metre lifting keel carrying 40 tonnes of ballast. The hi-tech sails are soon driving the sleek hull and Esense is starting to generate apparent wind speeds that are often greater than the true wind.

In photographs she can look almost dinghy-like with her simple, clear deck, but see Esense in the flesh and you marvel at her size and the 900 square metres of canvas that she carries. Her low aft deck, described as 'a terrace of the sea' and typical of Wally designs, is a vast area where owner and guests can recline and relax or dine in seclusion.

Esense is just as striking below decks. Luca Bassani, the designer behind Esense, has produced a yacht whose accommodation is almost infinitely flexible. Dining furniture can be moved from cabin to deck. Spacious reception rooms convert into well-appointed cabins. Galleys transform into cocktail bars.

Stylist Odile Decq has paired white upholstery and panels with dark wood floors and occasional flashes of orange. There's not a lot to hold onto in a seaway but the effect is stunning. The owner's stateroom boasts an en-suite bathroom as well as office and music room, and six guests can be accommodated in a further three cabins. The captain and four crew have their own less lavish living quarters.

The breathtaking attention to detail extends to the anchor – no hulking great bowroller for Esense. Instead the anchor is deployed invisibly from an underwater compartment and never breaks the surface of the water or spoils the lines of the bow.

And how about a carbon fibre toilet and bidet as the ultimate in bespoke construction and weight minimization? Esense is clearly 'heads' and shoulders above the rest.

BECOME PART OF THE BARMY ARMY

Follow a Caribbean cricket tour by yacht

Love sailing? Love cricket? Then what better way to spend an English winter than by following a tour of the Caribbean on your yacht. You'll be able to combine cruising and cricket in a way that will be the envy of anyone whose heart thrills at the sound of leather against willow and delights to hear a gurgling bow wave and a hissing wake.

The West Indies Cricket Board seems to bear the cruising audience in mind when planning the itinerary of international matches. Or at least it certainly did for the 2008 tour, which saw the four Test matches being held in a logical order that started in the north and gave enough time for cricket fans to recover from their post-match hangover and still reach the next ground in time for the toss. If future tours follow the same pattern, then you'll be in for a delightful cruise around the islands.

The First Test took place on the idyllic island of St Kitts, where the rich and famous still go to relax but where anchoring is free and the locals are famed for their friendly welcome. The Warner Park ground was one of many to be built for the 2007 Cricket World Cup. No east stand was built to allow the prevailing wind to cool the players and spectators.

You may have to battle that easterly breeze to reach Antigua for the Second Test but the passage isn't long and the port at Nelson's Dockyard is wonderfully protected. You'll be able to leave your vessel safely while spending the days at the Sir Vivian Richards Cricket Ground and enjoying the carnival atmosphere that's an integral part of cricket in this part of the world.

Next comes a longer hop to Barbados, but with the wind more on the beam you should enjoy some exciting sailing. If time allows you can island hop, calling in at such enticing places as Martinique and St Lucia.

The Kensington Oval was the venue for the Third Test and there are marinas at Port St Charles and elsewhere that provide a safe haven while you enjoy the pace and grace of Caribbean cricket played on home turf.

The last leg of this sporting odyssey was a downwind run to Trinidad for the Fourth and Final Test at Queen's Park. By the end of the tour, you'll have cruised almost the entire length of the Caribbean chain and undoubtedly seen some unforgettable cricket. With luck you'll also be able to catch some of the One Day International and Twenty20 games too. A cricket tour of the West Indies is the adventure of a lifetime and will earn you a place in pub discussions of sporting dedication for years to come.

category
races and rallies

location
South China Sea

difficulty
moderate

time
biennial

tempted by this?
try the Fastnet Race

RACE TO SOME FUN IN THE SUN

Sail hard and play hard in the San Fernando Race

The towering skyscrapers of Hong Kong make an impressive backdrop for the start of the San Fernando Race. The two-yearly event is a classic in the Asian sailing calendar and sees dozens of boats leave the busy city in their wake as they sail south to the sun and swaying palm trees of the Philippines.

The 770-km race was first held in 1977 and remains popular with sailors throughout the region. It is timed to coincide with Easter holidays and normally involves hard sailing and equally hard partying. The winds around Hong Kong can be unpredictable with typhoons a constant threat. The harbour is a major crossroads for international shipping and there is always a danger of collision. Once in open water the hazards do not cease. There are major oil platforms to which sailors must give a wide berth, although their blazing flames make a stunning sight in the middle of the South China Sea. Fishing boats are another hazard and closer in to the coast of the Philippines there is a small yet serious risk of piracy.

These eclectic hazards add some spice to a race that often includes some great ocean sailing with fresh winds and warm temperatures. Helming a yacht in the middle of the night with full sail up and the moon lighting up the ocean swell is a rare joy – especially when you can do so in your shirtsleeves.

The wind often drops as the fleet approaches San Fernando and crews tread their decks with care because any movement could slow the boat or spill wind from the sails. Brightly painted out-rigger fishing canoes flash past, the paddles of old now replaced by powerful outboards.

The town of San Fernando is a simple place. There is no marina and yachts must anchor in the bay, usually employing a local boatman to act as both water taxi and guard. Once ashore, it is easy to see why this event has such an unshakeable place in the hearts of local sailors. The beaches are lined with bars and the beer is a tenth of the price of Hong Kong. Not only is the beer cheap, the locals are very friendly and seem to welcome the influx of wealthy visitors.

The party starts when the first yacht crosses the line after several days at sea, and lasts long after the final finisher, days later. There is, however, more to the event than boats and beer. The San Fernando Race Foundation is a charity that raises money for an orphanage in the town and many children have benefited from the funds generated from this peculiarly Asian adventure.

category
voyages and destinations

location
Corsica

difficulty
moderate

time
all year

tempted by this?
try sailing into Sydney Harbour

SAIL THROUGH SOLID ROCK

Entering the harbour of Bonifacio is an awesome experience

A strong nerve and plenty of faith in your navigation is needed to approach Bonifacio. The entrance to the most southerly harbour on the Mediterranean island of Corsica is almost impossible to pick out from the deck of a yacht. You know where it should be but all you can see are the limestone cliffs that tower 70 metres above you.

With a compass in one hand – and the fingers of your other hand firmly crossed – you sail towards this solid, imposing edifice. You know that you must be close because on the edge of the cliffs are the houses and fortifications of the ancient town. Glancing up, you may wonder whether the inhabitants of those buildings are aware that the sea has undercut the rocks on which they are built, leaving them suspended dozens of metres above the waves.

Suddenly you see a fishing boat come around the headland – they must know how to find the way in. The breeze is rising and it's time to get out of the Strait of Bonifacio whose funnelling winds and scattered rocks and islands have claimed hundreds of sailors' lives. The fishing boat has vanished! It was there one second and gone the next. You sail towards the point where it disappeared and you suddenly see an opening in the cliff face and the entrance to the breathtaking and historic harbour that once sheltered Odysseus. Homer described it as 'a curious bay with mountains of stone to left and right' and nothing has changed.

Pass between these mountains of stone and swing round to starboard. Before you is one of the world's best protected ports, in which seafarers have sought shelter for millennia. The 12th century citadel that stands atop the cliff adds to the sense of security.

There's room to anchor in several small bays or why not moor stern-to at the town quay. A shouting Frenchman will indicate your allotted berth, though getting your boat into that spot may be physically possible. Argument is futile but don't despair, simply stick out your bottom lip, thrust your chin forward and lift your shoulders in the best Gallic shrug you can muster. This is French for 'Come off it mate!' and will result in being offered a more accessible berth.

Once ashore you'll have to climb the steep slopes into the old town, but then you'll be able to wander through the ancient town that marks the southern most point of 'Metropolitan France'. Look farther south and you'll see the Italian island of Sardinia – but don't expect pasta on the menu tonight. Bonifacio is French through and through so feast on the excellent food and relax, safe in the knowledge that your yacht could not be in a safer, or more spectacular, harbour.

SET SAIL ON A TALL SHIP

Climb the rigging if you dare

category
boats

location
worldwide

difficulty
tricky

time
all year

tempted by this?
try sailing like a Viking

Modern sailors have it easy. Today's yachts are equipped with sails that furl neatly away like giant roller-blinds and rigs that allow them to be sailed efficiently to windward. The two triangular sails of the Bermudan rig are a relatively recent invention and were preceded for hundreds of years by craft with fore-and-aft rigs that could not be sailed close to the wind. The largest of these vessels had dozens of sails and each one had to be set or stowed by a team of men who first had to climb the rigging then edge their way out along one of the yard-arms. It was hard and dangerous work and is now considered just the thing to give our mollycoddled youth an experience of true adventure.

The Sail Training movement is made up of organizations throughout the world that help all sorts of people experience the thrill of life aboard a Tall Ship. These giant vessels with traditional rigs require dozens of crew and teamwork is vital if they are to be sailed well. Crew have to take responsibility for their own safety as well of that of everyone else onboard. Add plenty of exercise and sea air and it is clear that this is an exceptional experience that can help teach that, with effort and cooperation, it is possible to achieve extraordinary things. It is a message that all sorts of people respond well too including the young and old, privileged and disadvantaged as well as the able-bodied and disabled.

In recent times, the term Tall Ship has been used to describe almost any vessel that is used for Sail Training. For most people, however, a Tall Ship is a craft with fore-and-aft rigging and there are some magnificent examples of these craft from all over the world. Uruguay, Greece, Canada, Indonesia, Mexico and Japan all operate Sail Training Tall Ships, as do America, Russia and many European countries.

Most of these vessels take part in a series of international events that involve long ocean passages and festivals of sail in port. The Tall Ships Atlantic Challenge that took place in 2009 is typical with dozens of craft and hundreds of crew sailing from Portugal to Tenerife, Barbados, Charleston, Boston, Halifax and back across the Atlantic to Belfast. These races and festivals present the participants with a real challenge and are a wonderful example of oceans bringing nations closer together rather than separating them.

RACE AROUND THE COAST OF FRANCE

Test your skill and stamina in the Tour de France à la Voile

The French love their sport, but oddly reserve a special place in their hearts for cycling and sailing, two activities that receive very little coverage in most other countries.

The highlight of the sporting calendar for both sailors and cyclists is the Tour de France, but whereas those on two wheels chase around the country using pedal power, the Tour de France à la Voile sees a fleet of yachts use the wind to race along the coast.

The course takes a fleet of identical yachts from the eastern edge of the Channel coast to the southern reaches of the Bay of Biscay. The 2009 event started in Dunkerque and involved six coastal legs to reach Royan, at the mouth of the Gironde River. Challenging coastal legs, of between 48 and 386 km included passages through the infamous Raz de Sein and Chenal du Four. Coastal sailing is interspersed with inshore sprints, ensuring that each crew's skills are tested to the limit. From Royan, the yachts were shipped overland to the Mediterranean where the racing continued with a further three legs before arrival in La Seyne-sur-Mer and the announcement of the winner.

The Tour de France à la Voile was first held in 1978 and has been a one-design event from the outset. Competitors race identical designs of boats and there are strict limits governing modifications and equipment. Six different yacht designs have been used over the last 30 years, with such famous names as the First 30 and JOD 35 being chosen because they represented the best balance between speed, seakeeping and affordability. The current fleet of Mumm 30s is due to be retired and a new design will first race in 2011. A competition to choose the next yacht received entries from 23 designers and builders, each eager to guarantee their reputation and income for years to come.

Each yacht has a crew of seven or eight and these tough sailors have to withstand a gruelling schedule with the event lasting almost a month and covering thousands of kilometres of intensive racing that inevitably includes some severe offshore conditions.

The race attracts some of Europe's best sailors and is a proving ground for those who want to reach the very top of the sport. Some boats are purely professional with the best of everything while others are raced by enthusiastic amateurs and students. Different classes allow keen competition whatever the level of financial support.

Each stopover is a cause for celebration and locals flood to the dockside to see these tough racers in their relatively small boats. Whereas the leading competitor in the cycling Tour de France earns the right to wear the yellow jersey, in this nautical version the special sponsor's spinnaker is flown with pride by the yacht that is at the top of the points.

SAIL AMONG WHALES

Mix wonder and worry
among these generally gentle giants

Whales not only live in the sea, they also embody its spirit. These mighty marine mammals are vast and mysterious with the ability to be both beautiful and wondrous as well as unpredictable and destructive. Watching a whale from a yacht under sail is always a thrill, though it can be a nerve-wracking business.

These mighty mammals can be bigger than your boat and yet have the power to launch themselves in the air and come crashing down, smashing anything solid that lies beneath them. Add strong protective urges to their young and you can see why sailors become a little nervous among whales.

It is possible to see whales in waters all around the world, though there are certain spots, at certain times of year, when a sighting becomes probable rather than unlikely. Pilot whales are frequently observed by sailors, but they are actually members of the dolphin family. Their behaviour is more whale-like and at up to 6.1 metres and 3 tonnes they are impressive, especially when seen in groups of up to 100 members.

The Humpback whale is a true whale, and at 15 metres is larger than most sailing boats. Humpbacks are acrobatic creatures that frequently breach, throwing more than half of their body out of the water before crashing down onto their backs. A whale must be swimming flat out to be able to breach and that can mean speeds of around 8 metres per second. If your yacht is in the way, you have little chance of escaping unharmed. Sperm, Humpback, Right and Gray Whales are all prodigious breachers, but other species also breach, including Fin, Blue, Minke and Sei.

There are recorded incidents of whales crashing down on yachts. A charter yacht in the Whitsunday Islands off Australia was badly damaged by a breaching whale though the crew were unhurt. Perhaps a greater danger is that a yacht collides with a whale and the keel or rudder is damaged. There have been many reports of possible whale collisions from the skippers of ocean racing yachts such as the Open 60s. When such sudden impacts are accompanied by blood in the water there can be little doubt that it was a sea creature rather than a log or submersed shipping container that did the damage. No effective solution to the risk of whale collision has been found, although yachts running their engines or operating sonar depth instruments are more likely to be detected.

Although whales can damage yachts, they are far more likely to be curious and have a quick look before disappearing with a flip of their giant tails. The sight of a whale alongside your yacht is something that you will never forget, nor is the phenomenal smell of fish from its blowhole.

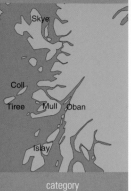

DODGE THE ROCKS AND HEAD FOR THE SCOTCH

Enjoy the ultimate Scottish booze cruise

category
races and rallies

location
Scotland

difficulty
moderate

time
14 days

tempted by this?
try the Eastern Med Rally

Sailors like their drink. It may be a tot of rum, a snifter of pink gin or a cold beer after a hard race, but a good day on the water is often celebrated with a glass of something. This combination of booze and boats is celebrated in fine style during the Classic Malts Cruise, which sees a small flotilla of yachts cruise the waters of Western Scotland, exploring the islands of the Inner Hebrides and stopping off at some remarkable distilleries along the way.

This annual event is all about scenery, sailing and scotch, with the whisky providing a good excuse to cruise in a truly spectacular setting where white sandy beaches fringe the shore and mountains form a stunning backdrop.

The fun starts at Oban where there's a chance to stock up on provisions before the first social function that is, of course, held at the Oban Distillery. The following morning there's a tour of the distillery that was founded in 1794 and produces whisky that blends the characteristics of both Highland and Island single malts, as is befitting from a town that stands at the 'Gateway to the Isles'. Having savoured the spice, sweetness, smoke and salt of the whisky, there's a chance to gather your strength for the sail to Carbost, a small community on the Isle of Skye and home to the Talisker Distillery.

The organizers ensure that there's plenty of time to discover some of the delightful anchorages that lie along the route of the Classic Malts Cruise. Skippers are allowed to go their own way, with some forming mini flotillas while others sail off in search of solitude.

The names of the lochs – Spelve, Sunart, Na Droma Buidhe and Moidart – give a feel of how other worldly this area is, where the drama of the surroundings can't be diminished by the rain that keeps the rolling hills so lush and green.

After four nights of exploration, it is time for the crews to reconvene for another tasting and tour. Talisker is the only distillery on Skye and one of the remotest in the whole of Scotland. The distinct peaty flavour of its whisky made it a favourite with Robert Louis Stevenson and there's plenty of opportunity to share some tales of the sea during the ceilidh and traditional Scottish supper that's held in the distillery's old cask store.

Next, the cruise heads south again with a myriad possible stopping points including Tinkers Hole, Iona, Bunessan, Loch Scridain, Staffa, Gometra, Ulva, The Tresnish Isles, Tiree and Coll. The final stop is at the Lagavulin Distillery on the Isle of Islay and there is a last challenge for those skippers who choose to pick their way through the rocks to anchor by the shores of this historic bay overlooking the ruins and Dunyvaig Castle. Less adventurous crews can moor their yachts at nearby Port Ellen and go by land to enjoy the farewell supper, tasting and tour. Participants of the Classic Malts Cruise always leave with promises to return to these stunning cruising grounds; they also set sail with a better understanding of the alchemy involved in turning water into whisky.

SURVIVE PIRATES

Sail through the Red Sea past modern day buccaneers

category
experiences

location
worldwide

difficulty
extreme

time
all year

tempted by this?
*try surviving in a
liferaft*

Pirates get a mixed press. There are the jovial, one-legged sort, with a parrot on the shoulder and a twinkle in the eye – or there are the modern variety with fast boats, rocket launchers and sub-machine guns. The first ones are great for children's parties and works of fiction, but the latter are becoming an increasing threat to sailors all round the world.

Acts of piracy are regularly reported in the waters of the Caribbean, South America, Africa and South East Asia. It seems that the temptation of a yacht is too great for some unscrupulous and possibly impoverished people. Modern cruising boats are likely to be carrying cash, computers, electronics and a variety of expensive boating equipment – and pirates know there will be minimal protection.

True piracy takes place in international waters; any form of robbery when anchored or closer to shore is legally viewed as simply theft. Whatever the definition, the fear is very real when your vessel is approached by an unknown boat in open waters. Modern pirates use high-powered open boats and can be upon you within minutes of becoming visible. Automatic weapons have replaced cutlasses and skippers are faced with a stark choice: fight or surrender?

Received wisdom states that you're better off handing over your valuables and escaping with your life, but there are some who believe that you should meet force with force. There is certainly no point in carrying a gun, however, unless you know how to use it and will be able to do so. Customs clearance of firearms is also highly problematic.

The most efficient defence is to stay clear of pirates altogether. This is best done by keeping well offshore, although fearless pirates do take their small boats far from land and sometimes operate from larger mother ships. Maintaining radio silence is also advised because pirates listen in to VHF radios, waiting to pick up on passing traffic. Travelling in convoy is also recommended. The site of a dozen yachts in a group will always be less appealing than a lone target. This is the policy adopted by some amateur round-the-world yacht races and rallies and sees vessels motoring instead of sailing so that they can stay close together. Also, a bare mast is less noticeable than unfurled sails to potential attackers.

If you're entering a risky area, consider splitting your possessions up and hiding them around the boat. Have some cash and other valuables that can be easily discovered, hopefully allowing the most precious and best-hidden items to stay safe.

South Africa

Cape Town   **Agulhas Current**

category
experiences

location
South Africa

difficulty
tough

time
all year

tempted by this?
try tackling the Portland Tidal Race

RIDE THE AGULHAS CURRENT

Face monster waves that snap ships in half

The eastern coast of South Africa is one of the world's most dangerous stretches of ocean. Fast moving water can collide with gale force winds to create giant waves, more than 30 metres high, which can break the strongest boat in two.

These monster waves are created when two powerful natural phenomena collide. The Agulhas Current is a thin band of water at the western edge of the Indian Ocean that draws its energy from the sun and accelerates southwards, reaching speeds of 5.8 knots. When conditions are kind it is a sailor's dream, whisking you along an ocean conveyor belt under blue skies. But danger is never far away.

To the south of South Africa lies Antarctica and the constant storms that rage around it. Areas of low pressure can drive upwards from these frozen wastes, with strong winds pushing large waves before them. When these gale-whipped waves collide with the Agulhas Current, all hell breaks loose.

The coming together of two irresistible forces creates 'wind over tide' conditions of epic proportions. Wave heights build and build until the crests tower dozens of metres above the troughs. This is not the mighty, rolling swell of a typical ocean storm. These waves rise like mountains and are tightly packed.

It is the steepness and the shortness of the sea that makes it so lethal. Tankers that stretch for hundreds of metres find themselves lifted into the air. With nothing to support their bow or stern they snap in two and are consumed in the boiling waters.

Look at the chart for the area and the warning is simple but clear: 'Waves of over 60 metres are experienced. Navigate with caution.' The situation is made all the more dangerous by the absence of somewhere to run and hide when the storms blow in from the south. The coastline offers little safety with long, surf-lined beaches interspersed with rocky outcrops. Great White sharks lurk beneath the water.

Yachts sailing around the world and opting to head for South America, rather than the Suez Canal and Mediterranean, frequently stop at Durban and are advised to wait for a good forecast before attempting the passage south. They should also take a thermometer with them and trail it behind the boat. The current is several degrees warmer than the surrounding water and it is useful to know when you are on the conveyor belt, or, if storms threaten, that you have got off it.

Survive the Agulhas Current and the Cape of Good Hope lies ahead. Beyond that Cape Town awaits, a safe haven where sailors have been welcomed for centuries.

FLY A HULL AT 40 KNOTS

Live life on the edge aboard an Extreme 40 catamaran

Imagine sticking your head out of a car window while travelling at 65 kilometres per hour. The force of the wind would be so strong that you find it hard to open your eyes or speak. Now imagine going at the same speed across the water, sitting on the hull of a catamaran that is flying 3 metres above the waves. That is the experience of the crews of the Extreme 40s who race in events around the world – and it is one that a few lucky VIPs get to share.

The Extreme 40 was dreamt up in an attempt to produce a sailing event that was accessible to the media and spectators. The catamarans are relatively uncomplicated machines that sail simple courses close to shore. They are spectacular to watch when going flat out and even more spectacular when something goes wrong. Measuring 12.2 metres long and 7.9 metres wide, they are capable of reaching speeds of up to 40 knots and will fly a hull in even moderate breezes.

This is a one-design class where all the boats are built by the same manufacturer and have identical equipment. This guarantees close racing and helps limit costs for sponsors. The length of the cats means that they can be transported in shipping containers, allowing the race circuit to take in a variety of international venues without incurring massive costs. The class attracts the best of sailors from all yachting disciplines, from dinghy to offshore racing. The possibility that the America's Cup could be competed for in multihulls led some of the best AC skippers and crew to take part, making the class a melting pot of exceptional talent.

The races are held as close to the shore as possible to give the viewing public a thrill and all judging takes place on the water so that penalties are instant and the boat that crosses the finish line first is undoubtedly the winner. Extreme 40s can be thrilling to watch and are so powerful and efficient that they can sail faster than the wind. Each cat has a giant downwind sail called a gennaker, which generates terrific speeds but can cause disasters and spectacular wipe outs known as pitchpoles. These happen when the hull in the water digs into a wave, causing the boat to somersault through the air, sending crew flying and possibly smashing the mast.

This is adrenalin-packet sailing and the four crew have to clamber from hull to hull across a giant mesh trampoline to keep the boat upright. To make their job even more difficult they have to look after a fifth crewmember, a VIP who is just along for the ride. This is corporate hospitality at its most adventurous and sponsors watch the racing with anxiety, hoping their guests have the ride of their life without being scared to death by the Extreme 40.

TAKE TO THE AIR
IN A MOTH

Rise above the waves in this extreme dinghy

It's small, it's very, very fast and it can fly. The Moth is a truly amazing sailing boat and is leading the way in hydrofoiling dinghies. This 3.35-metre craft that can lift above the water may seem extreme but the technology is likely to spread throughout the sport and all sorts of vessels will be able to take to the air in the future.

Moths can reach speeds of over 25 knots and their ability to rise out of the water is crucial because friction between the hull and the water is what slows boats down. The secret to a Moth's foiling abilities lies beneath the water. The centreboard is shaped like a long, thin upside down T. The horizontal foil is parallel to the hull of the boat but has a trailing edge that can be adjusted up or down, similar to the flaps on an aeroplane's wings. The rudder is also T-shaped with a foil and a flap, and it is the force of water passing over the trailing edges of these flaps that drives the boat upwards.

If the flaps are angled downwards the hull is pushed upwards and pioneering Moth designers had to overcome the problem of boats continuing to rise until the bottom of the centreboard cleared the water with disastrous results. The solution was a simple but ingenious device that automatically adjusts the angle of the centreboard flap. A thin batten extends downwards into the water from the front of the boat. The batten is connected to rods that adjust the angle of the flap. When water is flowing over the batten, the flap is angled downward and the hull is pushed up. As the batten clears the water it causes the flap is become more level and thus maintain the desired 'cruising altitude'. The helmsman can make further adjustments to fine-tune the centreboard flap and can also tweak the rudder flap by twisting a screw in the tiller.

It's a lot to think about when you're flying along at high speed, especially when you also have to keep the dinghy balanced by adjusting the sails and shifting your weight on one of the outrigger wings.

The Moth has experienced such radical developments because it's a development class where there are restrictions on dimensions but almost anything else is permitted. Innovation is welcomed and evolution is rapid because effective ideas are retained while those that never quite take off are allowed to sink.

The class first emerged in the 1920s and the less adventurous will be pleased to know that there are separate events for non-foiling and classic Moths.

category
voyages and destinations

location
Ireland

difficulty
moderate

time
44 hours +

tempted by this?
try sailing around the Isle of Wight first

CIRCUMNAVIGATE IRELAND

There are plenty of challenges whether you take the fast or slow option

The island of Ireland sits on the eastern edge of the Atlantic Ocean and offers rewarding sailing and a warm welcome to all yachtsmen and women who call at its shores. Given such a friendly reception – and the fact that circumnavigations have an undeniable appeal to sailors – it is strange that relatively few choose to complete a circuit of the Emerald Isle.

It may be the exposed western coast, where giant waves that build up over thousands of kilometres of open water come crashing against the cliffs. Perhaps it is the tricky tides and busy shipping of the Irish Sea, or could it be that sailors have such a good time at the first port they visit that they rarely sail much farther?

The challenge of circumnavigating the island is too great for some sailors to resist. Great names such as Sir Robin Knox-Johnston and Steve Fossett have held records for sailing non-stop around Ireland, Sir Robin doing so back in the summer of 1986 when his 18-metre catamaran, British Airways 1, completed the circuit in 76 hours.

The traditional non-stop race record starts and finishes off Kish Lighthouse in Dublin Bay and it was there that Fossett crossed the line onboard the crewed trimaran Lakota in 1993, taking a massive 32 hours off Sir Robin's record and covering more than 1100 kilometres at an average speed of 15.8 knots.

The crewed monohull record stands at 57 hours and was set in 2005 by the 18-metre CityJet Solune. Solo record attempts have been more numerous, mostly by amateur sailors on relatively small yachts. Michel Kleinjans holds the current record of four days and one hour, which he set in a 13.3-metre yacht in 2005. All these records are eminently breakable and it won't be long before a solo skipper aboard an Open 60 sets the bar considerably higher.

Of course there is an altogether more relaxed, if slower, way to sail around Ireland. Calling at a new harbour or port every night is a wonderful way to get to know a country and Ireland's varied coastline has challenges and delights in equal measure.

Time your trip to enjoy the competition of the Cork Week regatta, and then continue clockwise to sample the numerous gastronomic delights of Kinsale. There's Clear Island and the unmissable sight of the Fastnet Rock that lies beyond, before continuing round to Dingle and the dolphins that swim out to great you.

Ireland's western coast is its most dramatic but the exposure to the Atlantic and the scattered safe havens mean that a good forecast and a healthy sense of adventure is required. In return you can enjoy some of the most beautiful and unspoilt waters in Europe and be sure to see a wide array of fascinating sea life.

There are plenty of interesting coves and rivers to explore along the northern coast as well as some stunning beaches, and don't forget to ride the tide up to scenic Strangford Lough as you head south on the homeward leg through the Irish Sea. With endless cruising opportunities it seems a shame to fly around this island jewel in just a few days.

category
*voyages and
destinations*

location
Pacific

difficulty
moderate

time
all year

tempted by this?
*try visiting the Cape
Verdes*

CRUISE THE GALAPAGOS ISLANDS

Sail through an ecological wonderland

Pass through the Panama Canal on a round-the-world sailing adventure and your first stop in the Pacific is likely to be the Galapagos Islands. This group of 13 main islands, six smaller islands and 107 rocks and islets was made famous by Charles Darwin who used the archipelago's isolation to help support his theory of evolution. The oldest of the islands is thought to have emerged from the sea more than five million years ago, whereas the youngest islands are still being formed, with volcanic eruptions as recently as 2008.

Darwin's visit onboard The Beagle took place in 1835 and the wildlife is still varied and unique. The young naturalist's observations that mockingbirds, finches and tortoises differed from island to island formed a crucial part of his evidence supporting the theory of natural selection. The ecology of the islands has not been without human interference however. British pirates, who used the archipelago as a base from which to attack Spanish ships laden with gold, introduced goats as a supply of fresh meat. The Spaniards responded by setting dogs loose to eat the goats and so deprive the buccaneers of a food source.

The islands are located on and around the equator and some 972 km east of the South American mainland. They are governed by Ecuador whose officials take the archipelago's recognition as a UNESCO World Heritage Site very seriously. Visiting sailors have received a mixed welcome over the years. The pioneering adventurers were left to explore the islands with few restrictions, but growing ecological awareness and a realization of the income that could be generated caused attitudes to change.

There was a period when yachts where seen as being more trouble than they were worth and were discouraged from visiting, allowing the authorities to concentrate on the more profitable and easily managed tour ship and charter flight tourists. Those attitudes have changed and sailors are once again free to visit, although they must call into one of the main ports, such as those on the islands of Isabela, San Cristobal and Santa Cruz.

The paperwork that needs to be completed and the money that needs to be paid differ from port to port and official to official. It is possible to apply for a permit to visit some of the outlying islands by yacht though an official park warden has to accompany you. Overnight stops at these islands are also possible, although they are extremely expensive. These high charges pay for the preservation of the wildlife and prevent ecological damage by overuse – nonetheless they can jar with sailors who are used to the freedom of the seas.

An alternative is to take one of the local cruise boats, either on a general tour or on a private charter.

RACE AROUND
THE WORLD NON-STOP

Compete in the Vendée Globe, the ultimate sailing challenge

category
races and rallies

location
worldwide

difficulty
extreme

time
84 days +

tempted by this?
Try the Volvo Ocean Race

The Vendée Globe is known as the Everest of sailing, but this doesn't do it justice. Climbing the mother of all mountains is certainly hard and extremely dangerous but hundreds more people have stood atop Everest than have sailed solo and non-stop around the world.

The yacht race known simply as The Vendée is named after the region of France where it starts and sees a fleet of brave men and women sail into the North Atlantic at the start of a three-month sprint around globe. They sail Open 60 monohull yachts that are built with speed rather than safety as a priority. The designers will disagree, but the number of dismastings, keel failures and ripped sails is undeniable evidence that these vessels, just like Formula One cars, are built to be fast and not to last.

The Vendée course is simple. Head south from the start at Les Sables d'Olonne and then east around the Cape of Good Hope at the tip of Africa. Keep going around the world until you see Cape Horn to port then head north, back up the Atlantic to where you started. Skippers will cover between 40,000 and 43,000 km before the finish and have to pass through a series of imaginary gates to keep their course clear of the worse of the icebergs that drift up from Antarctica into the Southern Ocean.

Dodging icebergs is just one of the many problems that Vendée skippers must overcome. Sail changes on these 18.2-metre yachts take a superhuman effort and trips to the top of the towering mast are routine. The boats may be big but they lack almost all creature comforts in an effort to reduce weight and maximize speed. A bucket replaces a toilet and dog bowls are used for crockery. Food is dried and some skippers drink neat vegetable oil in an attempt to load up on calories as efficiently as possible. An average of five hours sleep a day is maintained during the three months the sailors are at sea.

Modern communication means that these solo sailors must become authors and TV stars as well as driving the boat as quickly as possible. Blogs must be updated and video broadcasts beamed back via onboard satellite systems. There is also constant maintenance and more than a third of the fleet usually drop out because of failures of boat or equipment.

The race takes place every four years and although the most modern boats cost many millions of pounds, it is possible to buy one of the older generation boats for a fraction of the price. You need a sponsor to help fund the refit and new sails will be essential, but you can be assured of plenty of help from the special band of fellow solo ocean sailors. You're unlikely to win in an old boat, although recent races have shown that the tortoise is often more likely to finish than the hare.

category
*voyages and
destinations*

location
Australia

difficulty
moderate

time
all year

tempted by this?
*try cruising the islands
of Halong Bay*

CRUISE
THE WHITSUNDAYS

There are at least
74 good reasons to sail Down Under

Think of a sailing paradise and images of white beaches, secluded bays, clear water and lush tropical islands may well spring to mind. Those images probably bear an uncanny resemblance to the Whitsunday Islands off the eastern coast of Queensland in Australia. There are 74 islands in the archipelago with countless bays and inlets to explore.

One of the many things that makes the Whitsundays internationally famous is the colour of the sand. White silica beaches fringe the shore of the islands that were once the peaks of mountains before sea levels rose millions of years ago. To the east lies the Great Barrier Reef which encloses the Whitsundays. The reef, one of the world's greatest natural wonders, protects the islands from the ocean swell of the Pacific, ensuring relaxed sailing in azure waters.

The best known spot on the Whitsunday Islands is Whitehaven Beach, a vast expanse of sand that makes it the most photographed beach in Australia. It's a must-see but is also on the itinerary of every tripper boat in the area. For the adventurous sailor there is so much more to these islands and exploration is well rewarded. Only eight of the 74 islands are inhabited, leaving numerous beaches and bays as natural havens.

The spectacular sea life is not limited to the Great Barrier Reef and masks and snorkels are essential kit for any sailor. Some charter yachts are also equipped with scuba gear and there is plenty to see beneath the sea. Most spectacular are the humpback whales that visit the area every year between June and October and can be seen rocketing out of the water in spectacular breaches. Don't get too close and make sure that you don't come between a mother and her calf or the splash may be replaced with a smash. Another fascinating creature that only the fortunate will see is the dugong. This large marine mammal lives on sea grass and is an endangered species.

The Whitsundays is an area to explore at a gentle pace, stopping at such places as Plum Pudding Island, Hook Island and Butterfly Bay. Few non-Antipodean sailors are able to reach these wonderful waters in their own boats, but there are plenty of charter companies that can provide all sorts of craft, from small yachts that you can skipper yourself to racing catamarans that skim across the water with dozens of backpackers onboard.

However you choose to sail these waters, you can be certain that the memory will stay with you for a very long time.

Baffin
Island

Canada

category
voyages and destinations

location
Arctic

difficulty
extreme

time
summer, northern hemisphere

tempted by this?
try sailing to South Georgia

SAIL ACROSS THE TOP OF THE WORLD

Attempt a crossing of the Northwest Passage

Sailing from one coast of North America to the other via the icy expanses of the Arctic is something that has fascinated mariners for centuries. It is a challenge that only the most adventurous sailors set themselves, and though not impossible, failure is far more likely than success.

The Northwest Passage is the sea route through the Arctic Ocean that joins the Atlantic and Pacific oceans. It has been a Holy Grail for centuries especially after Pope Alexander VI decreed in 1493 that Africa and South America were to be split between Portugal and Spain. This left nowhere for northern European ships to stop on their way to trade in Asia and prompted King Henry VII of England to send ships in search of a way through the ice. Explorers tried to find an east to west route for hundreds of years and although they succeeded in mapping much of this virgin territory, they failed to find a passage. Explorations were being mounted at the same time to find a way through from the west, but these too all failed in their ultimate goal.

In 1775, the British government offered a staggering £20,000 prize for the first person to discover this prized sea route and brought Captain James Cook out of retirement to seek the elusive, and at this point only theoretical, Northwest Passage. Despite Cook's expertise and the size of the reward, the expedition was unsuccessful.

It was only in the first half of the 19th century that ships ventured north of the Bering Strait and towards the real Northwest Passage. Of the many explorers who charted those waters, it is widely acknowledged that Sir Robert McClure discovered a route through, though it was not then navigable. More expeditions followed and some were caught in the ice with the loss of all crew, either through starvation (and subsequent cannibalism) or lead poisoning from tinned food.

It was the great Norwegian explorer Roald Amundsen who first took a ship through the passage in 1906, though the journey took three years. The feat was not repeated until 1940. More ships followed and transit times reduced, although the problems of shallow waters and ice that can quickly trap a ship means that the route was never considered an important one for commercial vessels.

In 1977, a Belgian yachtsman named Willy de Roos sailed through the Northwest Passage in his 13.8-metre steel yacht Williwaw. The first true 'sailing' with no engine power was in 2007, when French sailor Sébastien Roubinet journeyed from coast to coast in his specially designed 7.5-metre catamaran, which could sail on the ice as well as through the water.

Ice has always been the biggest challenge to sailors wanting to pass through the Northwest Passage. Tragically, the task seems to becoming easier as global warming causes the melting of the polar ice caps. It may be that this once almost-impossible route will become an ocean thoroughfare rather than the reserve of the most daring adventurers.

CHARTER THE WORLD'S LARGEST SLOOP

Just don't sail her under any bridges

category
boats

location
worldwide

difficulty
moderate

time
all year

tempted by this?
try chartering a J Class

For those who believe that bigger is better, there's nothing quite as good as Mirabella V – the world's largest single-masted yacht and a sight to behold. Launched in 2004, she's 75 metres long and her mast towers 89 metres above the deck, although that does prevent her from passing beneath the Golden Gate Bridge. In fact, at 100 metres from keel to masthead, she's twice as tall as Nelson's Column.

The creation of such a large single rig shattered conventional wisdom about the limits and loads that a yacht could withstand. Mirabella's winches can pull 40 tonnes, her 1.5 tonne mainsail contains 26-metre battens, she carries 15 tonnes of 76-millimetre-thick rod rigging, and her keel weighs 150 tonnes. The mast may limit her cruising grounds but the keel lifts to allow her access to ports that would otherwise be off limits.

Her huge hull and gargantuan sails, balanced by a keel that weighs as much as 100 saloon cars, means that she sails quickly. In fact she is quicker under sail than when driven by her huge engines and can keep pace with most motor-driven superyachts.

Mirabella V is capable of speeds of up to 20 knots under sail, although her massive scale means the sensation for those onboard is reassuringly sedate. All sail-handling equipment is operated by a mixture of hydraulics and electronics, meaning that the small crew has finger tip control.

In addition to the 8.8-metre Hinckley Picnic Boat, the yacht's 'toys' include snorkelling, scuba and water-ski equipment, four Laser sailing dinghies, personal water-craft, kayaks, rowing skulls and remote control sailing models of Mirabella V. A gymnasium and sauna are located on the yacht's lower deck.

Mirabella V provides the option of dining on the 'sky deck', the covered cockpit or, more formally, in the main dining room that can seat up to 20 guests. Take your time over the wine list because the cellar contains 600 bottles of the best vintages.

After dinner you can view a film under the stars on the yacht's large outdoor projection screen, complete with full surround sound wireless headphones, or relax in the Jacuzzi dip pool on the foredeck.

Owner Joe Vittoria made his fortune when he sold the Avis car rental empire, but he charters Mirabella V out to recover some of the US$50 million building costs. A week on board for you and 11 friends costs US$400,000 in low season, though you may have to pay harbour fees of US$2,000 a night on top of that. Plus there's the 10 percent tip!

Suffolk
Orford ●

Essex

Chatham

Kent

category
*voyages and
destinations*

location
UK

difficulty
moderate

time
all year

tempted by this?
*try exploring the Golfe
du Morbihan*

DISCOVER THE MAGIC OF THE SWATCHWAYS

Sail the UK East Coast shallows on a shoal draught adventure

The waters around the Thames Estuary look like unpromising sailing territory. Strong tides turn meandering rivers to ribbons of mud and transform apparently open sea to far-reaching sandbanks that lie in wait for unwary sailors. There must, however, be something special about the place as thousands of yachtsmen and women call this place home and many of them would rather sail here than anywhere else on the planet.

It is hard to appreciate the joys of cruising the East Coast without first hand experience. There is something intangible about the beauty of the mudflats and marshes that defies description. The inhospitable nature of the mud and shifting sands means that humans have not been able to build, modernize and so spoil the area. Hordes of tourists in search of white sandy beaches or towering cliffs pass this stretch of coast by, leaving it almost entirely for sailors to enjoy.

Of course it takes a special breed of sailor to enjoy the space and solitude of the East Coast. Boastful boaters may prefer to stick to the Solent where there's always a chance to see and be seen, a wealth of yacht clubs and a lively après-sail scene. The mudlark sailor knows that the tide is the boss and accepts that exploring these waters is often a literal case of 'going with the flow'.

And what waters they are to explore! Between the sand and mud lie swatchways, narrow channels that are navigable around high water but become impassable when the tide ebbs away. These shortcuts through the sand were traditionally marked by withies or saplings, though some are now buoyed. The strong tides that sluice through them cause the sands to shift and going aground is an inevitable part of the East Coast experience.

Many yachts have been designed with these shallow waters in mind and twin bilge keels or lifting keels are common among the craft that cruise here. Rivers are interspersed along the coast, providing plenty of boltholes and ports of call. The Swale and the Medway lie south of the Thames while the Roach, Crouch, Blackwater, Colne, Stour, Orwell, Deben, Ore, Alde and Blyth lie to the north.

Each has its distinctive character and many are rich in maritime history. Sail up the Medway to Chatham and you'll be following in the wake of countless ships of the line that were based at the naval docks. Harwich is still a busy port but beyond it is the River Orwell whose delightful wooded banks run through peaceful countryside until they reach the city of Ipswich.

Farther to the north is Orford and one of the most difficult river entrances along this frequently challenging coast. The shingle banks that lie at the mouth of the Orford River move so much that an annual survey is taken to plot their position and help sailors pass safely and enter calm waters before continuing upstream for a pint of East Coast beer at the Jolly Sailor Inn.

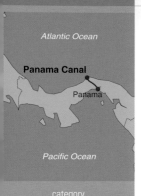
category
experiences

location
Central America

difficulty
moderate

time
all year

tempted by this?
try cruising the French canals

TRANSIT THE PANAMA CANAL

Cross a continent while shadowed by giants

The Panama Canal is a mere 80 km long but it takes you from one side of the world to the other. It is one of the greatest engineering feats ever accomplished and some 27,500 lives were lost during its construction. To transit the Panama Canal is an adventure in itself and for many sailors marks the start of a Pacific cruise about which they will have fantasized for years, if not decades.

The French first attempted to build a canal between the Atlantic and Pacific in 1880 but malaria, yellow fever and the sheer scale of the task defeated them. An American project was started at the start of 20th century and the canal was finally opened in 1914. It was now possible to take a boat from one side of the USA to the other without circling Cape Horn and the whole of South America.

The landmass that the canal cuts through is 69 km wide as the crow flies and reached a height of 95 metres before the engineering works started. A kink in the Central American isthmus means that the canal runs southeast from the Atlantic to the Pacific, not due west as one might imagine.

The canal was designed for international cargo vessels and the largest of these that can still make the transit are described as Panamax boats. It is into this world of ocean leviathans that humble yacht skippers must venture, putting their fragile fibreglass or wooden hulls into an environment of rusting steel, coarse concrete and vicious currents.

To transit the canal yachts must be able to motor at least 4 knots or a tow will be required. They also need four mooring lines of at least 38 metres and at least four adult crew to handle these lines, in addition to the skipper. Crews waiting to transit the canal often volunteer to act as deck hands on other yachts and so know what to expect when the time comes for their crossing. Long lines, extra fenders and additional crew can all be hired at both ends of the canal. A pilot or transit advisor has to be carried on board.

Yachts up to 15.2 metres are charged US$500, though there is also a deposit to be paid and the complicated bureaucracy involved in obtaining permission to cross can involve extra payments. The transit itself involves passing through three sets of locks as well as several artificial lakes and a 12.6-km cutting. Fast yachts can complete the passage in a day though slower vessels will have to anchor overnight in one of the lakes.

As adventures go it is undoubtedly both stressful and industrial – it is also quite unforgettable.

category
races and rallies

location
Caribbean

difficulty
moderate

time
April

tempted by this?
try Cowes Week

HAVE A RUM TIME IN THE CARIBBEAN

Sail hard and party hard during Antigua Sailing Week

Warm sun, fresh winds and clear blue sea – the Caribbean is a yacht skipper's paradise and many sailors flee the cold of the European winter to cruise among this chain of islands and compete in the growing number of regattas and races.

One of the premiere events is Antigua Sailing Week, a regatta that attracts a fleet of almost 200 yachts, including some of the biggest boats from throughout the region as well as dozens of international craft that come to compete and have fun in the sun.

The event takes place at the end of April and traditionally starts with a 'feeder race' from the neighbouring island of Guadeloupe. The racing then lasts for six days and involves a variety of courses to test the skills of skippers and crews. Races are held off the island's south and southwest coasts and a particular highlight is the round-the-island race for the bigger boats that compete in Class A. There really are some very big boats with giants-of-the-ocean such as the 30-metre ICAP Leopard and 27-metre Rambler doing battle among the Caribbean swell. These are some of the fastest yachts on the planet and their multimillionaire owners choose Antigua Sailing Week as the venue to settle old scores from other classic races such as the Fastnet and Sydney-Hobart. Such giant craft battle it out with TP52s, Swan 601s and other top notch yachts, all with red hot crews. The biggest boat is normally first over the line, but it is the corrected time that counts and an intricate handicapping system allows an eclectic mix of yachts to compete against one another.

Multihulls have made a welcome to return to the start line in recent years and trimarans and catamarans of all shapes and sizes compete in their own classes. Lightening quick 18-metre tris do battle against more modest 9-metre vessels, whereas the exciting class of Gunboat performance cruising catamarans is growing every year. There are even four classes for charter yachts where everyday boats with amateur crews enjoy extremely tight competition.

Racing is at the heart of the event but crews find time to party too. There are some legendary evening events during the course of Antigua Sailing Week and crews' stamina is tested to the limit as they sail hard and play hard.

Many charter companies offer boats and berths for hire and there are opportunities to get afloat in everything from fully-crewed Open 60s to more modest Swans; or why not charter your own 'bareboat' and skipper your own yacht in an exciting regatta with a distinctly Caribbean character.

category
*voyages and
destinations*

location
Indonesia

difficulty
moderate

time
all year

tempted by this?
*try exploring the
Galapagos Islands*

GO SAILING WITH THE DRAGONS

Cruise and dive the waters of the Komodo National Park

Sail eastwards from Bali for 320 km and you enter the Komodo National Park. It's a stunning area that can only be explored by boat, with plenty of adventures on offer both above and below the sea.

Officially declared a World Heritage Site in 1991, the Komodo National Park encompasses 132,000 hectares of marine waters, making it one of the largest protected zones in the world. The area boasts one of the world's richest marine environments with over 260 species of coral, 70 species of sponge and over 1,000 species of fish, marine reptiles and mammals.

Sailors who explore these waters often do so aboard yachts specially equipped for diving, with the delights of the deep including pygmy seahorses, anglerfish, manta rays, dolphins, whales and dugongs. Some yachtsmen and women set out to sail the world and ensure that their craft will double as a dive boat, whereas others book a berth onboard one of the stunning sailing craft that are based around this beautiful corner of Indonesia.

In this part of the world boats are still built by hand from wood and the charter vessels are works of art, combining traditional techniques with luxurious interiors. Ironwood and teak are among the raw materials used by the master builders on islands such as Sulawesi and the craft are usually variants of the gaff-rigged pinisi boats that have traded throughout the region for centuries. The pinisi is a fascinating blend of East and West with a hull similar to that of a junk and a fore-and-aft rig more commonly found in Europe. The first pinisi ships are said to have been based around the designs of the Dutch pinnace craft that sailed these waters in the 17th century.

Whatever yacht you are on board, no trip to the region would be complete without a visit to the island of Komodo, made famous for the dragons that dwell there. These fearsome animals are the largest lizards in the world and can grow up to 3 metres long and weigh more than 70 kg. Their diet consists mainly of carrion although they will hunt living prey including birds and mammals. An extraordinary sense of smell allows them to locate a dead or dying animal from a distance of 9.5 km. The Komodo dragon can swallow a goat whole, though may take 20 minutes to do so. After digestion, it regurgitates a mass of horns, hair and teeth covered in malodorous mucus.

Cruising the Komodo National Park is a true feast for the senses and sailors can witness amazing sights every day. With tropical islands, crystal clear waters and a wealth of natural wonders, it really is the place to go for an ecological adventure.

WANDER THE WORLD IN A WAYFARER

The capable cruiser that shows that size doesn't count

Adventurous sailors are in the habit of attempting extraordinary passages in very ordinary boats. The greatest proponent of such low-key adventuring is Frank Dye, an Englishman with a small Wayfarer dinghy and a huge amount of nerve.

The Wayfarer was designed by Ian Proctor in 1957 and at 4.82 metres long was large enough to accommodate three adults or numerous children and therefore popular with sailing schools. There was also a very active racing circuit and Wayfarers still compete all round the world. The simple plywood construction meant that numerous boats were homebuilt and the large, flat floor space provided room for two people to lie flat. This unusual feature encouraged owners to camp in their Wayfarers, rigging a tent over the boom.

With sleeping arrangements taken care of, the possibility of longer cruises was explored. Enthusiastic sailors took their Wayfarers farther and farther afield, taking advantage of watertight lockers to stow essential camping kit. Various modifications are required before a standard Wayfarer is ready to be sailed offshore. Most important of these are the changes to the mainsail to allow it to be reefed in strong winds. A battery and navigation lights need to be installed if there will be any night sailing and some skippers add an outboard engine to prevent being becalmed in shipping lanes.

These tough little boats soon proved themselves to be capable of handling tough conditions. Frank and Margaret Dye, owners of Wanderer W48, showed what these craft are really capable of. Frank completed numerous open water passages and made a 1040-km voyage in 1963 from Kinlochbervie in Scotland to Iceland, enduring gale force winds on the way. The following year he and crewmate Bill Brockbank sailed from Scotland to Aalesund, Norway, surviving four capsizes and a broken mast during a Force 9 storm.

The example Frank set has inspired thousands of other Wayfarer sailors to try their hand at cruising in an open dinghy, as well as attempting open-water passages of hundreds of kilometres. There are Wayfarers sailing in waters all around the world and their low cost and simple design has ensured their popularity for more than 50 years. New boats are still being built and raced and there is a large second-hand market with plenty of bargains to be had.

Anyone considering some Wayfarer cruising is well advised to read the Dye's account of their adventures – and with titles including 'Sailing to the Edge of Fear', it is clear that life onboard can be far from plain sailing.

category
races and rallies

location
Mallorca, Spain

difficulty
moderate

time
August

tempted by this?
try Cowes Week

COMPETE FOR THE KING'S CUP

Sail with royalty in the Copa del Rey

The King's Cup is a true highlight of the Mediterranean sailing calendar and attracts some of the best sailors from all around the world. The setting is the historic city of Palma, capital of the island of Mallorca, and it is an area blessed with almost perfect sailing conditions.

The summer weather is reliably hot and by early afternoon the sun has warmed the land enough to create a fresh sea breeze that blows all afternoon across the Bay of Palma. A variety of yachts compete in a mixture of one-design and IRC handicap classes, and competition is fierce throughout. The focus of the attention is on Juan Carlos, the King of Spain, who competes onboard his TP52 with a crew of professional sailors frequently seen on America Cup yachts. The King is no royal playboy who's just along for the ride – he's a highly skilled sailor and represented Spain in the Dragon class during the 1972 Olympics as well as in Admiral's Cup events. His son, Prince Felipe, is also a regular Copa del Rey competitor.

To campaign a TP52 competitively requires a seriously big budget, but there are opportunities for extremely close racing in yachts where you don't have to break the bank to be the best. The X-35 is a great example of one-design racing where strict rules govern the yachts, crew and equipment. With these regulations creating a level playing field, the speed of the boat comes down to the skill of the crew and fleets are always tightly packed from start to finish. These 10.5-metre yachts are built in Denmark, and although intended primarily as racers, they are also built to be comfortable cruising boats. More than two dozen of these one-design pocket-rockets do battle each year and the size of the boat is no reflection on the competitors will to win.

The weeklong Copa del Rey event is based at the Real Club Nautico de Palma and there is plenty of après-sailing activities as the super-rich sailors enjoy the trappings of their wealth. Many will have brought their superyachts to Palma to act as floating apartments.

The event – which should not be confused with football tournaments in Spain and Thailand that have the same name – was first held in 1982 and has ridden the waves of rating wrangles and recessions over the years. The organizers know that to remain a leading regatta they must change with the times and cater for the fast changing pace of yacht design and innovation. It is this willingness to keep the Copa del Rey open to the most exciting yachts – combined with the fantastic setting and great climate – which ensures that the annual fight for the Kings Cup will continue for many years to come.

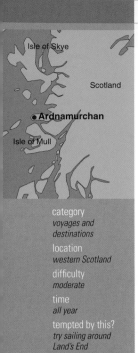

category
voyages and destinations

location
western Scotland

difficulty
moderate

time
all year

tempted by this?
try sailing around Land's End

BRAVE THE WATERS OF BRITAIN'S MOST WESTERLY POINT

Sail around Ardnamurchan and you'll have 'earned the heather'

Glance at a map of the British Isles and you're likely to declare Land's End as the most westerly point on the mainland. Take a closer look and you'll see that actually the headland of Ardnamurchan in Scotland holds the title.

Ardnamurchan extends 37 km farther to the west than its Cornish competition and shares its reputation as somewhere that only adventurous yachtsmen and women will gladly sail. The headland seems protected by the islands of Coll, Mull and Muck that lie around it, but another close look at the map shows that it's totally exposed to the North Atlantic, which sends great waves to crash upon the boulder-strewn shore. The power of the ocean swell is magnified by the uneven seabed that churns up the water into a boiling nautical nightmare.

So what draws sailors from the relatively sheltered cruising grounds of the Sound of Mull and Firth of Lorn that lie to the south? Solitude and scenery are the answers, for the waters around the isles of Skye, Rhum and Eigg are spectacular but make for challenging sailing. The Point of Ardnamurchan acts as a gateway and those that sail beyond it earn the privilege of flying a sprig of heather from the bow of their vessel when they make the return journey. It is a rite of passage that has existed for centuries and is still observed today.

Most yachts heading north start their passage from the colourful town of Tobermory, now famous to television-watching toddlers as Balamory. You'll need to time the trip to make the most of the north-running tide and keep a good eye out for the rocks known as The Stirks that lie off the entrance to Loch Sunart. If white water is breaking on The Stirks you're well advised to turn back.

If the wind is light, it is possible to stay close to the coast and pass beneath the Ardnamurchan lighthouse, a column of granite 55 metres high. If the breeze is fresh then steer well clear of the coast, passing at least 3 km to seaward and clear of the most disturbed water. Go too close and waves as large as houses tower above you – it's no place for anything but a well found yacht and an experienced crew.

Once beyond the point you'll be able to enjoy the stunning scene that lies ahead with islands and inlets and whisky galore. But beware, the passage home can be even more testing, and that's why only the boats that return earn the heather and wear it with pride.

Atlantic
Ocean

Cornwall

Azores

RACE TO THE AZORES – AND BACK

The Azores and Back is the perfect amateur adventure

category
races and rallies

location
Atlantic Ocean

difficulty
tricky

time
15 days +

tempted by this?
try entering the San Fernando Race

Decide to sail around the world and you'll need hundreds of thousands of pounds and a couple of years. Opt for a circuit of the Atlantic and at least three or four months are required. Sail to the Azores (and back) and you'll get away with it by taking all your holiday in one go and begging a week or two of unpaid leave.

The Azores and Back Race, universally referred to as the AZAB, is a proper adventure. It is for single- and two-handed sailors and involves spending 7–10 days on the open ocean on both the outward and homeward legs.

The idea for the race came about when, in 1972, a letter was published in *Yachting Monthly* magazine calling for a solo ocean race that was shorter than the current transatlantic 'OSTAR' event. The editor, Andrew Bray, met with Spud Spedding and Colin Drummond and came up with the idea of racing to the Azores. Colin had links to the Royal Cornwall Yacht Club and so Falmouth became the starting point.

The first race took place in 1975 with 52 starters and the organizers then decided to run the AZAB every four years. The 1979 event was opened to yachts with two crew as well as solo skippers, and now nearly all entries are in the two-handed class. Sailing 'two-up' makes life much easier during sail changes and allows for companionship during changes of watch.

The course from Falmouth to the Azores is almost due southwest. The coastline of Cornwall must first be cleared and AZAB yachts have been known to go aground on Black Rock, the one hazard in the Falmouth Harbour. Once clear of the Lizard Peninsula, there is nothing but open water until landfall at the Azores, a group of Portuguese islands some 1500 km west of Lisbon.

The route takes the fleet directly into the prevailing winds and these strong winds can kick up monstrous seas as the yachts cross the plateau where the relative shallows of the English Channel drop off into the massive depths of the Atlantic. The route steers clear of the major shipping lanes but there is always a danger of collision. The organizers recommend that all yachts are equipped with a radar alarm system and radar target enhancer. This is compulsory for yachts sailed single-handed.

The Azores have only been inhabited since 1439 and the nine islands are now home to more than 200,000 people. Exploration of their lush and often mountainous interiors is highly recommended after making landfall at Ponta Delgada, on the island of São Miguel.

GET TO GRIPS WITH 18 FEET OF PURE ADRENALIN

Try your hand at Aussie Rules sailing

For the ultimate in one-hulled thrills and spills there is nothing, absolutely nothing, like an 18ft skiff. These ultra-demanding dinghies are strictly reserved for those with the highest level of skill and the greatest nerve. With giant sails and light hulls they skim across the water, often on the verge of becoming airborne and frequently wiping out in epic style.

The 18ft (5.5 metres) skiff is at the cutting edge of modern sailing but has a long and glorious history that stretches back for more than a century. Sydney Harbour in Australia was the setting for the first 18-footer races when slim wooden boats, each carrying between 18 and 25 crew and flying up to seven sails, did battle on courses close to shore.

The class was the invention of Mark Foy who wanted to make sailing a popular and accessible spectator sport. He succeeded and the class took off, though the size of sails and crews was reduced to limit costs. In 1935 a new league for these smaller boats was formed and their popular appeal was such that seven ferries full of spectators would follow the races each weekend.

Modern 18ft skiffs are still sailed on Sydney Harbour and the thrills and spills are recorded by helicopter TV crews and broadcast all over the world. The appeal of these craft is so enduring because they have always pushed the limits. The designers have constantly challenged the boundaries of possibility and the ratio of sail area to boat size is truly extreme, allowing skiffs to plane across the water in relatively light winds. If the breeze gets up then they really take off, flashing over the waves with the constant threat of disastrous capsizes and pitchpoles.

The minimum crew of three dangle from trapezes, with their feet resting on the edges of wings that extend from the hull to help balance the boat. Lightening reactions are required to keep the skiffs upright and great strength is needed, along with quick footwork to dash from side to side during tacks and gybes.

Restrictions on hull design help to limit costs and the philosophy of the class is to provide 'good, fair, close racing' as well as 'enjoyment for all competitors'. The fact that the 2009 Sydney Harbour championships were decided on the final race with four skiffs crossing the line within six seconds of each other suggests that the class continues to uphold the ideals of Mark Hoy.

There's no room for passengers on modern skiffs but a healthy class of historic skiffs does exist. These boats have crews of more than six and so allow non-elite sailors to experience the thrill of these 18ft flying machines.

England

English Channel

France

CROSS THE ENGLISH CHANNEL

Dare you sail across some one of the busiest shipping lanes in the world?

The English Channel is a giant funnel, directing shipping from the Northern Atlantic into a stretch of water that, at its narrowest, is just 6 km across. More than 400 commercial vessels pass up and down the Channel every day and a Traffic Separation Scheme separates ships moving in opposite directions.

The captains of the craft that use the Channel are constantly working against the clock. The sooner they can offload their cargo, reload and set to sea, the more money they will make. Speed is everything and slowing down on changing course costs them money.

It is into this hectic world of maritime commerce that you must venture if you wish to sail from the British mainland to the coast of France. Your small craft will disappear in the troughs of waves and its fibreglass hull is unlikely to show up on the radar screens of the ocean leviathans that tower dozens of metres above the waves.

With a speed of only five or six knots, you are at the mercy of these giant ships as you try to cross the west-bound and east-bound shipping lanes. You must pick your gap carefully, estimating the speed of the other vessels and hoping that they keep a steady pace.

The rules that govern the crossing of shipping lanes are aimed to ensure that yachts spend as little time as possible on these marine motorways. Skippers must cross at right angles and are obliged to stay clear of those using the lanes. It is easier said than done because yachts are limited in their heading by the direction of the wind.

When crossing, use a hand bearing compass or radar to monitor the relative position of vessels that may present a collision hazard. If the angle between you and them remains the same, you are likely to collide. Collision regulations detail exactly what each boat should do if the worst is about to happen. Early avoidance is key and always remember that it can take many minutes for these giant craft to change course whereas yachts can change direction in the blinking of an eye.

The shipping lanes cover the narrowest and busiest stretches of the English Channel but there is no room for complacency when sailing anywhere in these waters. There may not be another vessel in sight but, travelling at around 20 knots, it will take less than 15 minutes for a ship to appear from over the horizon and reach your position. Constant vigilance is essential, and never forget the fruits de mer and cheap booze that await across the Channel.

ROUND CAPE HORN

Join the select few who have rounded 'The Horn'

There are few landmarks as iconic as Cape Horn. The rocky edifice marks the southern-most tip of South America and sailing around it is the greatest adventure that some sailors can conceive.

The Cape is not part of the continental mainland but an island, several kilometres across, which forms part of an archipelago. Photographs taken from the sea show nothing but a barren edifice rising from the foaming seas of the Southern Ocean, although the island is actually covered in vegetation.

Cape Horn marks the division between the Pacific and Atlantic Oceans and has been legendary since the first explorers felt their way through these storm-whipped waters in the 16th century. The Horn soon earned a reputation for high seas and incredibly strong winds and though it became part of the global shipping routes, it would regularly extract its toll in sailors' lives. Conditions at Cape Horn are so severe because the wind and waves of the Southern Ocean have to pass between South America and Antarctica, which lies just 650 km to the south. The might and ferocity of the Roaring Forties can be concentrated in the treacherous waters beyond the Cape, though there are periods of calm when the famous headland shows a gentler side.

Rounding Cape Horn is an integral part of any non-stop circumnavigation and for many sailors marks the start of the final leg. The rise in recent years of round-the-world racing has brought the mythical cape back into sailing lore and there is a growing demand among leisure sailors to round Cape Horn.

The waters around the cape and among the islands, inlets and outcrops of southern Chile are a natural paradise. They may be cold and wet but they are also hardly touched by human hand and wildlife abounds, along with natural spectacles such as glaciers running down to the sea.

A dedicated group of charter skippers spend the southern summer sailing these waters in their sturdy steel yachts and offer the chance to sail around Cape Horn as part of the package. Guests will pay thousands of pounds for their time onboard, in addition to the cost of airfares to southern Chile.

The season lasts from October to May but weather conditions are unpredictable and days of rain are not uncommon. Navigating the thousands of channels of Patagonia and Tierra del Fuego is a hazardous business, with hidden rocks and williwaw winds that rush down the hillsides and appear from nowhere. Small Antarctic cruise ships do visit these waters but to be a true 'Cape Horner' you need to transit this far flung rock under sail.

category
races and rallies

location
Palma, Mallorca

difficulty
moderate

time
June

tempted by this?
*try chartering the
Maltese Falcon*

RACE WITH THE RICH AND FAMOUS

Enjoy the wonder of wealth at the Superyacht Cup

Superyachts are an almost compulsory status symbol for the super-rich. These craft cost tens or even hundreds of millions of pounds and can have dozens of crew on board. They sail the world's oceans, providing luxurious accommodation and exciting sailing from Sydney to the Solent and Cannes to the Caribbean.

Up to 70 superyachts sail to Palma on the Mediterranean island of Mallorca each summer to take part in the Superyacht Cup. The event allows the rich and famous to race against one another and enjoy lavish hospitality. A vast, purpose-built Superyacht Cup Village incorporates VIP lounges, stylish bars, chic restaurants and an entertainment area. The gleaming yachts are moored along the dock allowing visitors to catch a glimpse of these incredible craft.

They may boast marble bathrooms with gold taps and be equipped with saunas and cinemas, but superyachts were designed to be sailed. Brash billionaires spend their cash on powerboats but the soulful super-rich splurge on sailing boats and love to see them being sailed hard.

A handicapping system allows different shapes and sizes of craft to compete and staggered starts are organized to ensure tight finishes. They also minimize the risk of collisions as skippers jockey for position before the starting gun.

The very latest designs such as the ultra-modern Wallys share the water with best designs of yesteryear. The growing fleet of elegant J Class yachts has added the Superyacht Cup to its calendar and other beautifully restored classics grace the Bay of Palma as they compete in the fresh breeze that appears every afternoon.

Some of the best professional racers join the regular crews who are more used to sailing in cruising mode and ensuring that the guests' cocktails aren't spilt. With hydraulic sail handling systems to take the strain, these giant craft can be pushed hard and no quarter is asked for or given once the races are underway. The sight of so many massive yachts racing together is without its equal and spectator boats are crammed to the gunwales.

The three days of competition are interspersed with evening events when owners can compare notes and discuss plans for the winter cruising season in the Caribbean. In fact, the popularity of the Superyacht Cup in Palma has led to the creation of a sister event that takes place in Antigua at the end of the year. The event is based at Nelson's Dockyard and the sight of so much perfectly polished brass and immaculately swabbed decks would have delighted the British sea commander who based his fleet in this protected bay. Caribbean sailing conditions are as reliable as those in Palma and good winds, warm waters and sunshine ensures an enjoyable event.

Entry to the Superyacht Cup is open to all multimillionaires with super-sized yachts and a love of racing.

BATTLE THROUGH
THE BALTIC ISLANDS

Test your body and mind
in the Archipelago Raid

The concept of the Archipelago Raid is simple: to visit 25 checkpoints by boat and return to the starting point. A quick glance at the 100,000 islands that are spread across the racecourse and the true scale of the task starts to become clear. Add to this the fact that the checkpoints are spread over hundreds of square kilometres and the sailors are on the water for 15 to 18 hours a day on board small open catamarans, and you have a recipe for one of the most gruelling sailing events in the world.

The Archipelago Raid takes place around mid-summer among the islands of the Stockholm, Åland and Finnish archipelagos in the Baltic Sea. Up to 35 teams take part in the six-day, almost 1000-km event, each with a Formula 18 catamaran sailed by a crew of two. These open cats are incredibly fast but are difficult to sail well and easy to capsize. In strong winds one of the hulls will lift out of the water and both crew dangle in harnesses on the end of trapeze wire to keep the boat upright.

It's this combination of high-adrenalin sailing and intense navigational challenges that makes the event so demanding. Competitors are not told how best to get between checkpoints and so have to pick their way between rocks and islands, hoping that the wind stays steady. If the breeze does die, the pair of paddles that each crew carries can be used to keep the boats moving, making this a distinctly different sort of sailing race.

Crews camp at the end of each exhausting day's sailing before being given the positions of the checkpoints for the next day's racing. One hot meal a day is provided but all other food must be carried onboard, along with tents and all maintenance equipment, because outside assistance is forbidden.

There are wide stretches of open water to cross as well as intricate inshore navigation, and crews finish the event battered and bruised. Ellen MacArthur took part in the 2008 Raid and had to stick a red-hot needle through the fingernail of her teammate to pierce a painful blister below. This is not a race for any but the toughest sailors.

The Archipelago Raid attracts an incredibly diverse fleet with international offshore yachtsmen and women competing against Olympic catamaran sailors and hardened extreme adventurers. The challenge is both physical and mental with sleep deprivation and exhaustion taking its toll, usually in the form of capsizes and collisions with the numerous rocks that turn the race into a hazardous and extremely adventurous assault course.

Acknowledgements and further reading

West Country Cruising; Mark Fishwick, Wiley Nautical

French Canal Routes; Michael Briant, www.michaelbriant.com

117 Days Adrift; Maurice Bailey, Adlard Coles Nautical

Wight Hazards, Solent Hazards; Peter Bruce, Boldre Marine

Crossing the Line: Tradition, Ceremony, Initiation; C Swartz, US Navy

With thanks

To those who made suggestions on the www.ybw.com forums.
To David and Judy Williams for allowing me the opportunity to write.
To Daisy for all the biscuits.
To the wonderful team at Wiley Nautical, especially David, Drew and Claire.